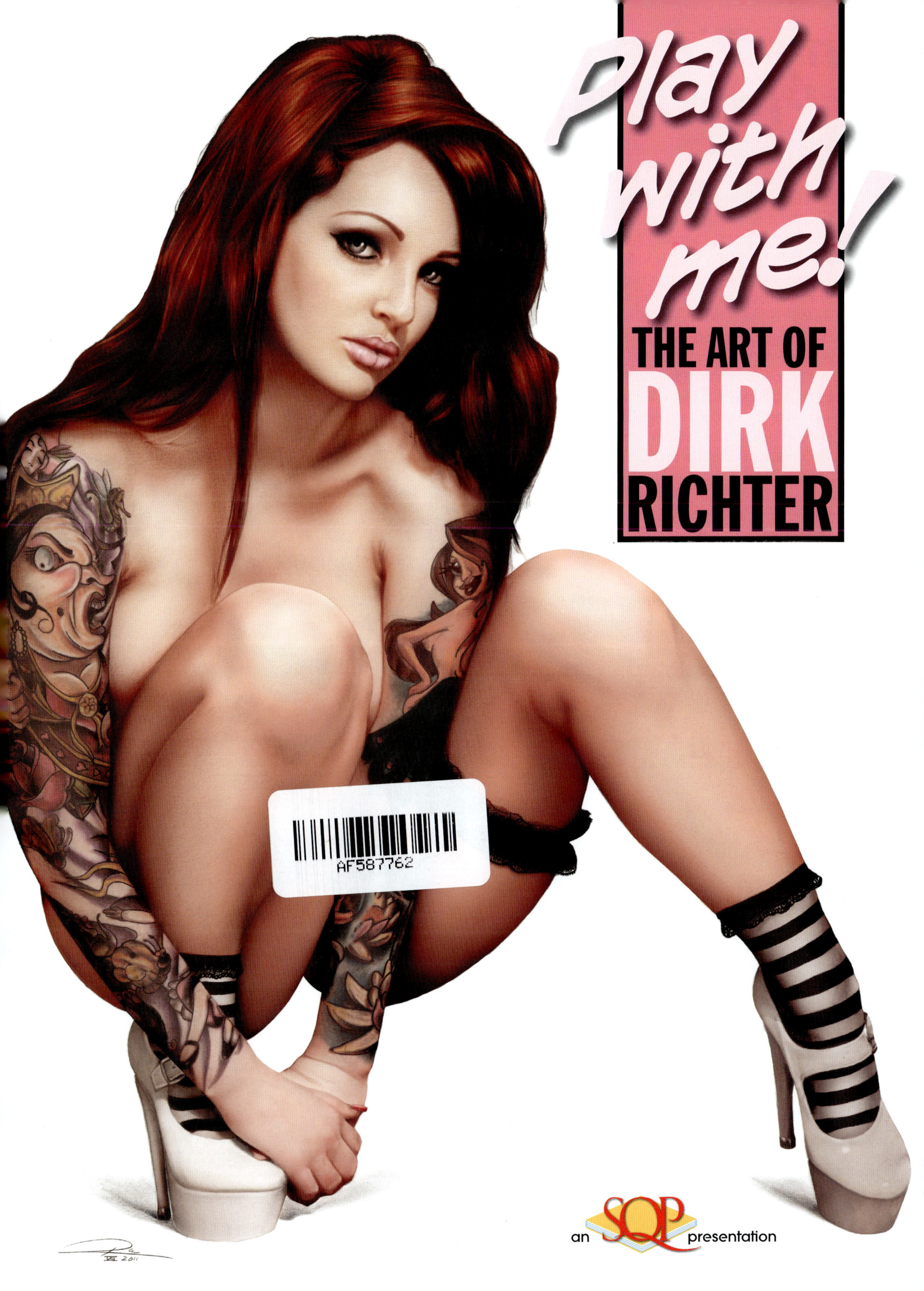
Play with me!
THE ART OF
DIRK
RICHTER
an SQP presentation

Any Time is Playtime!

DIRK RICHTER AND THE ART OF BLISSFUL DELIGHTS

Intricate, intimate, and inviting would best describe the sensual illustrations of Dirk Richter. Inspired by such modern-day titans as Oliva de Berardinis and Hajime Sorayama, as well as photography great Robert Alvarado, Richter strives to bring each one his luxurious ladies to life. For over ten years, this self-taught artist has been following his fascination with the female form with loving determination. Often spending well over 50 hours or more on each piece, he brings the requisite realism a pinup naturally demands, along with a smoky sexuality and playful attitude. It's a formula that's gained him international respect and showcases all around the globe.

Born and raised in Germany, Dirk currently lives in Hannover, and continues to create new illustrations for his many followers. For the very latest on his work, go to:

www.dirkrichterart.com

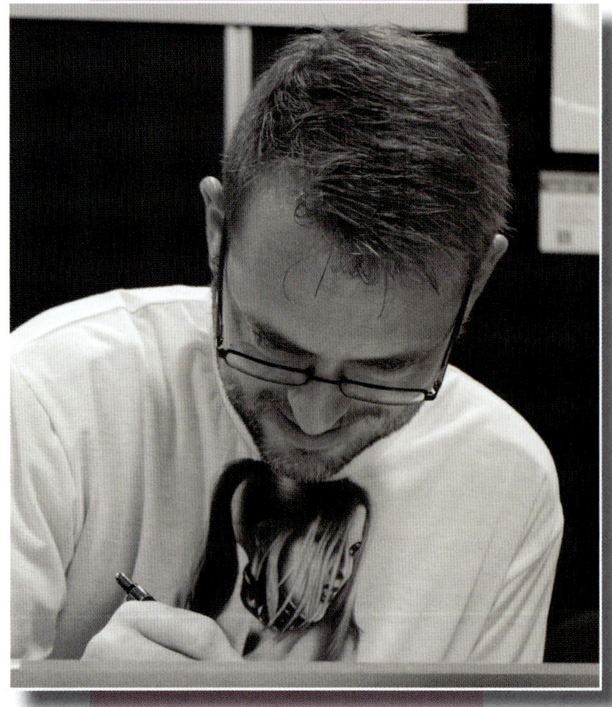

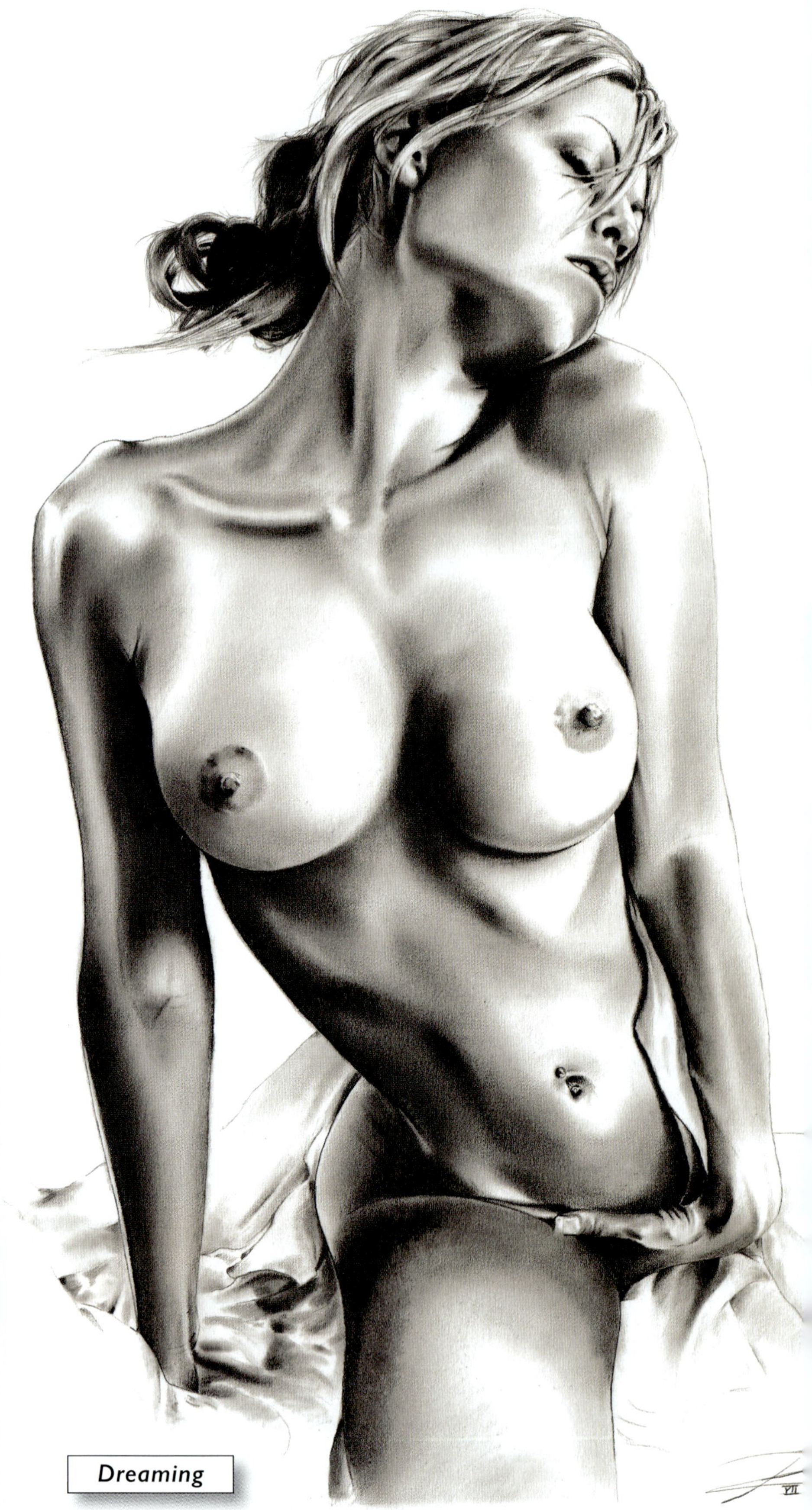

Dreaming

Play With Me - The Art of Dirk Richter

Book design by Grassy Knoll Studios.

Published by SQP Inc. - PO Box 248 - Columbus NJ 08022

Sal Quartuccio & Bob Keenan - Publishers

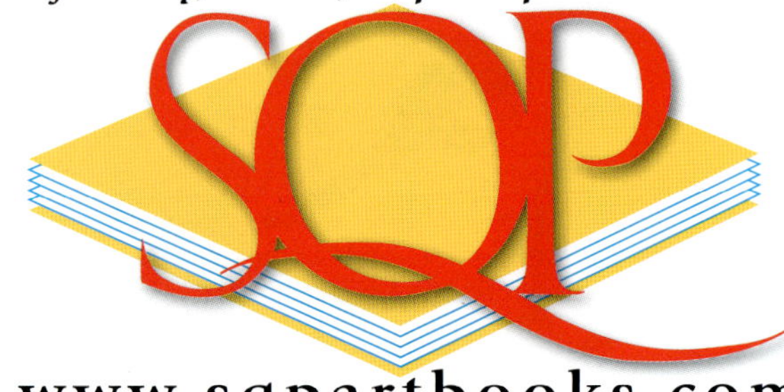

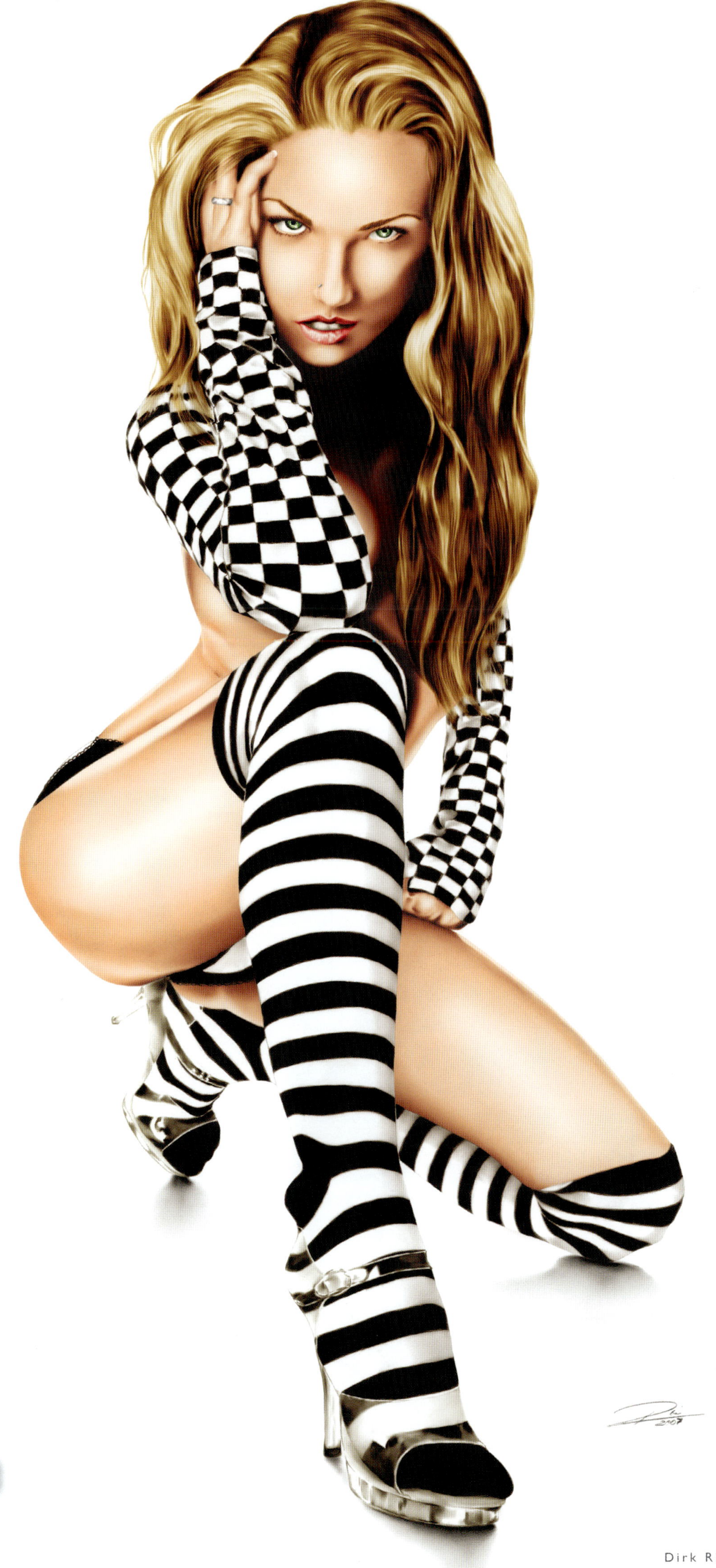

Checkers

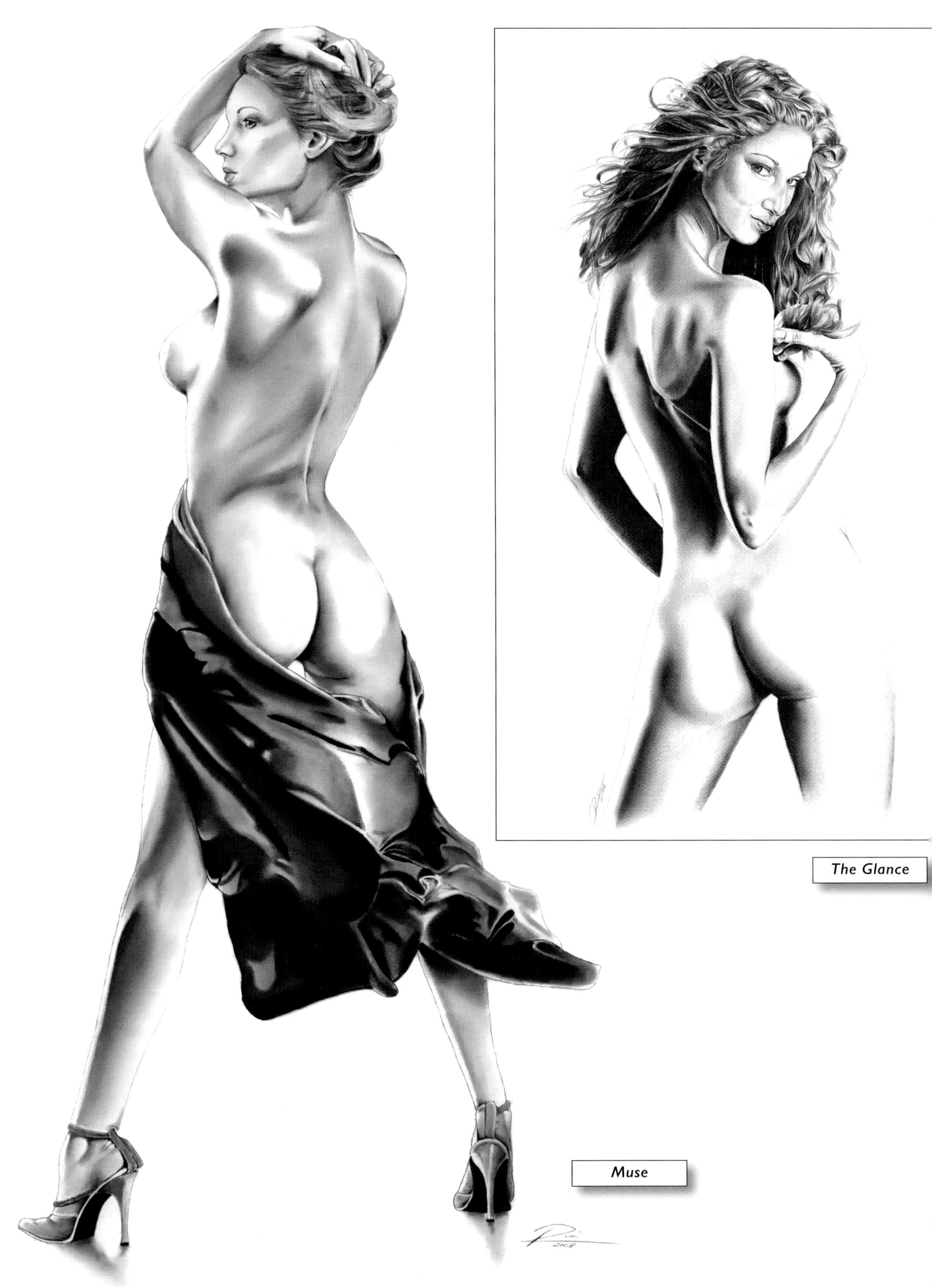

The Glance

Muse

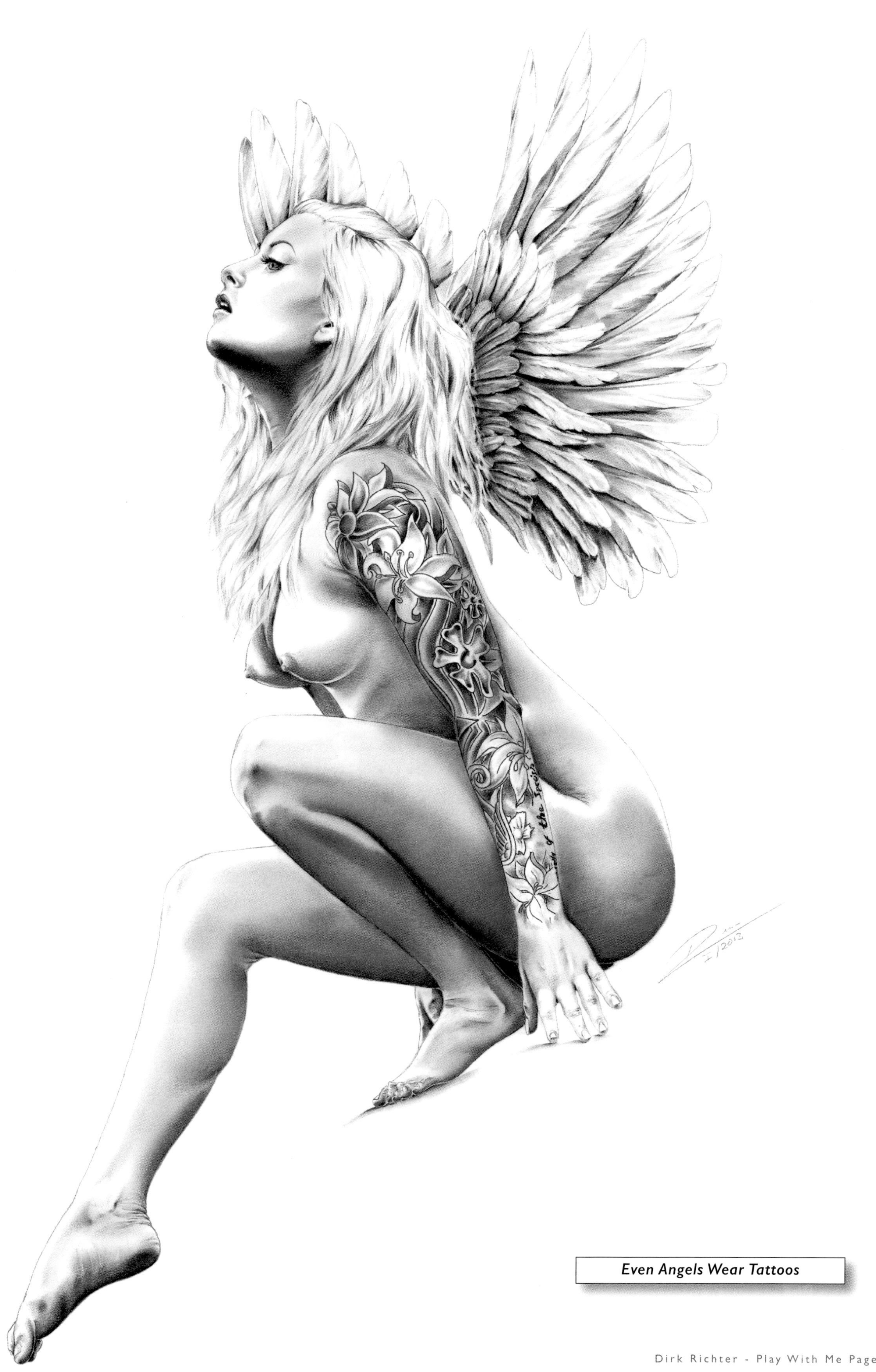

Even Angels Wear Tattoos

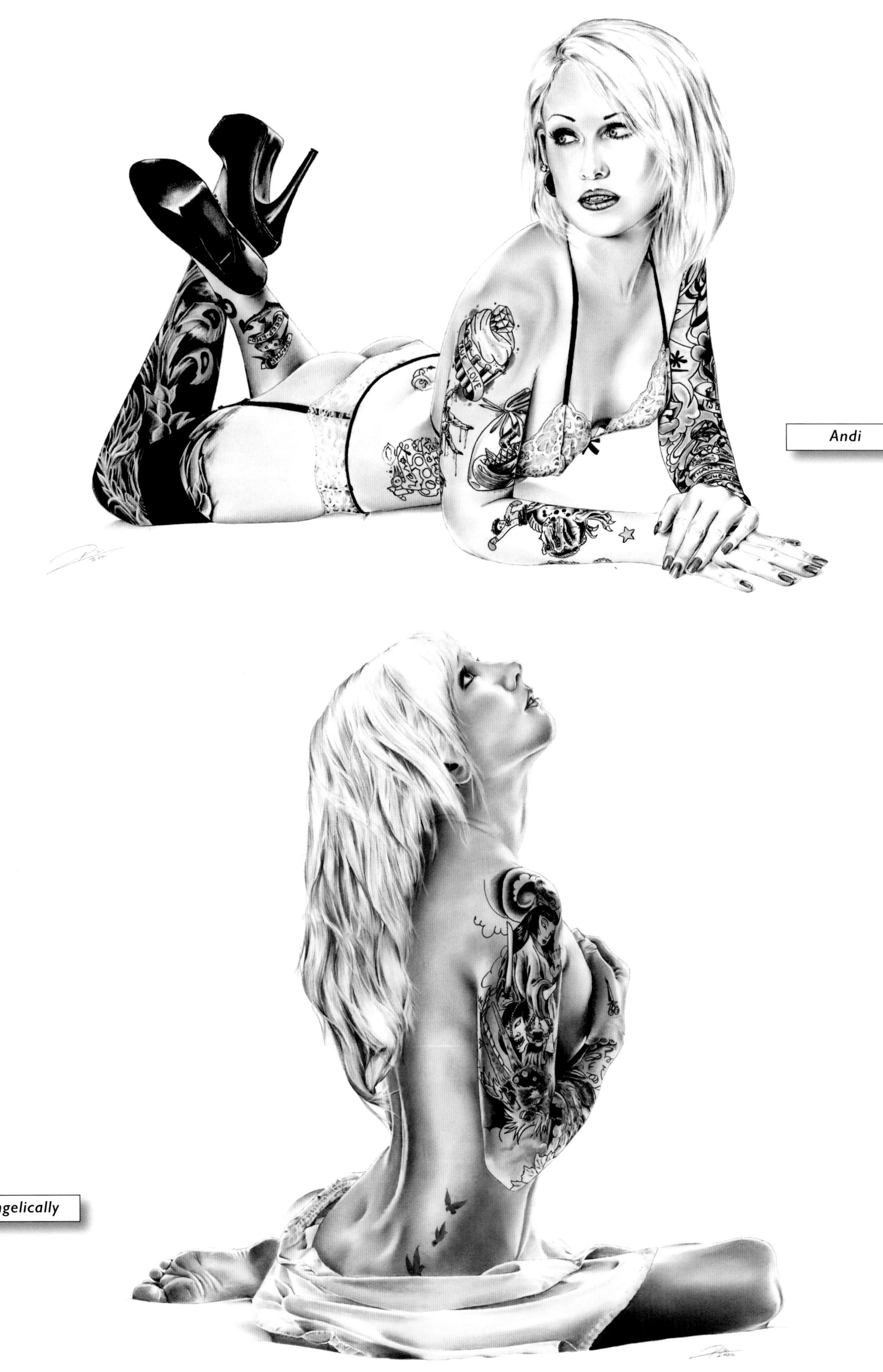
Andi
Angelically

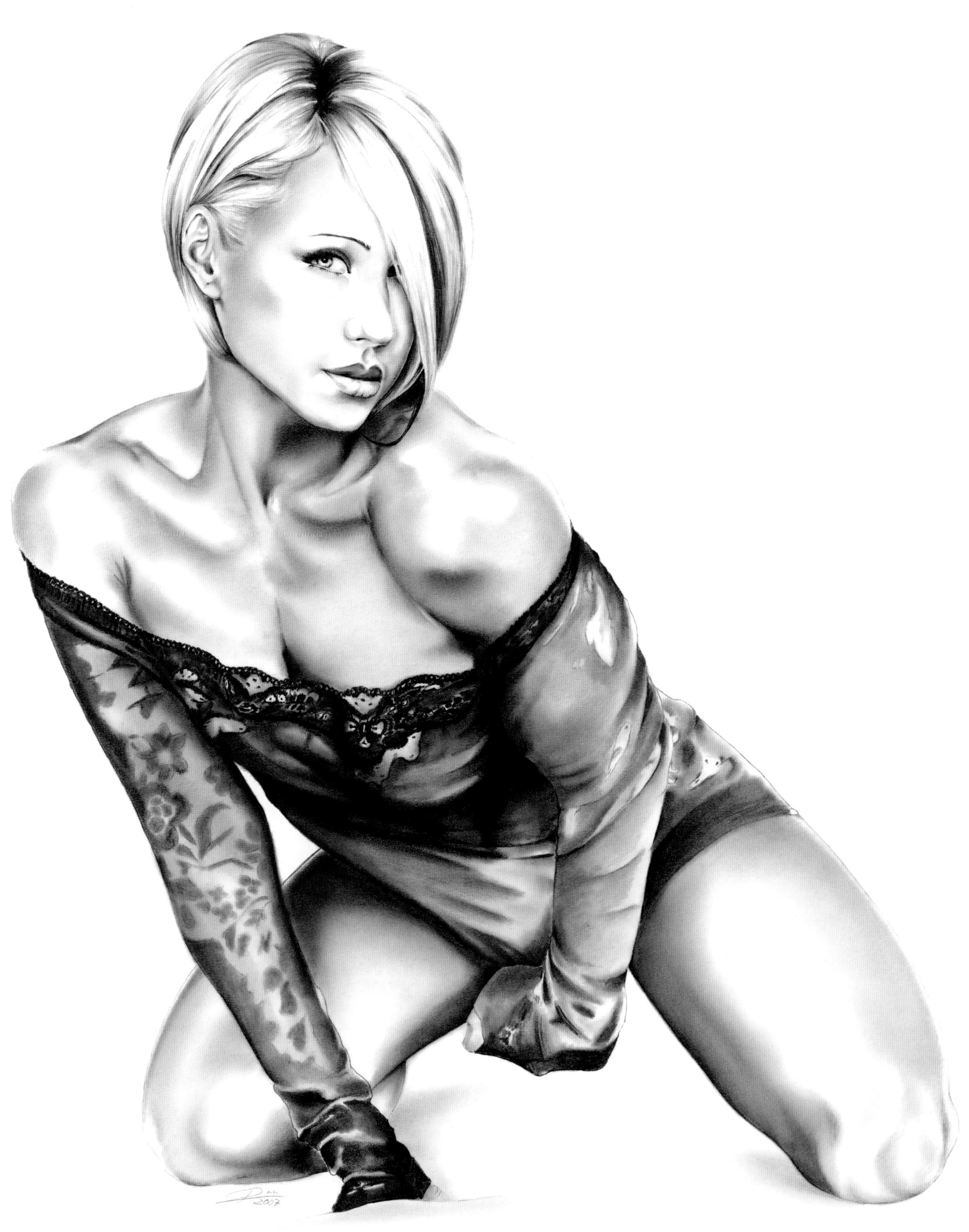

Bashful

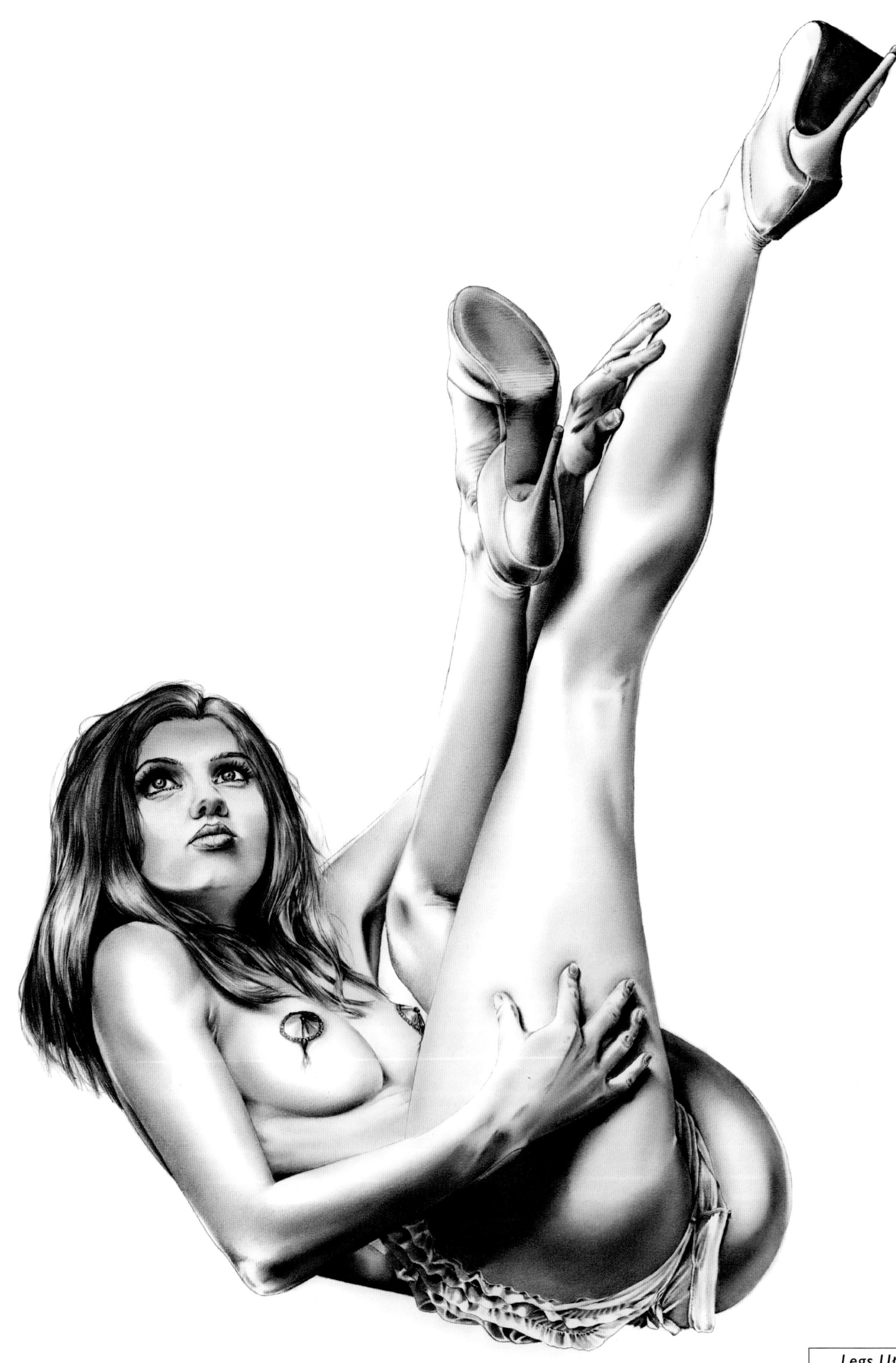

Legs Up

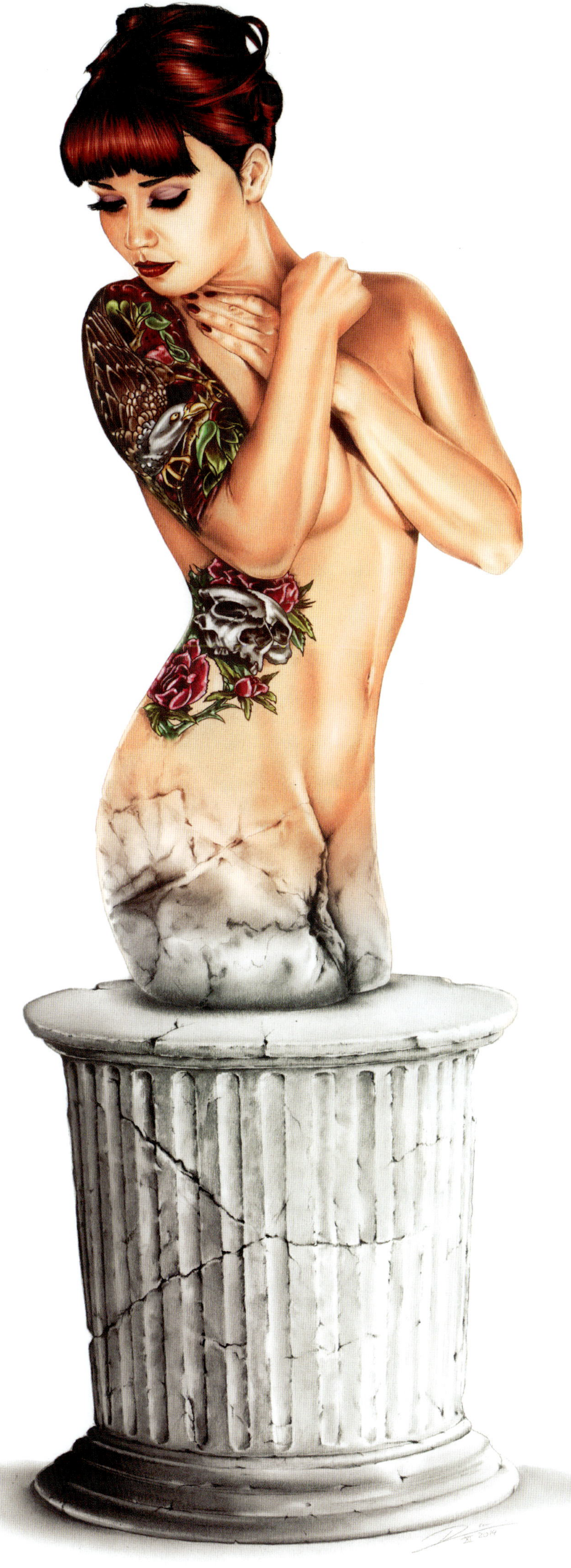

Serenity Trapped

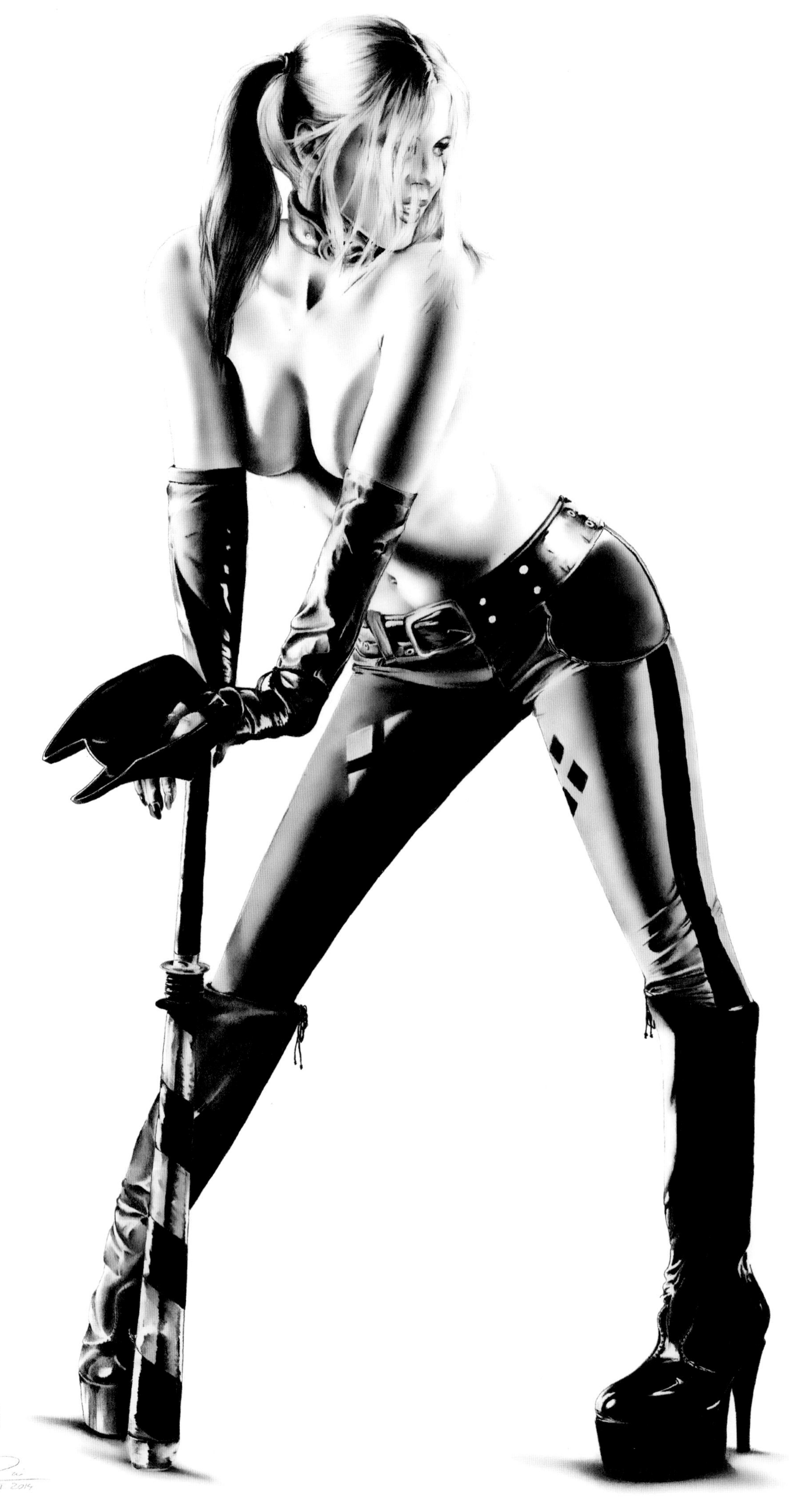

Bat Her Up

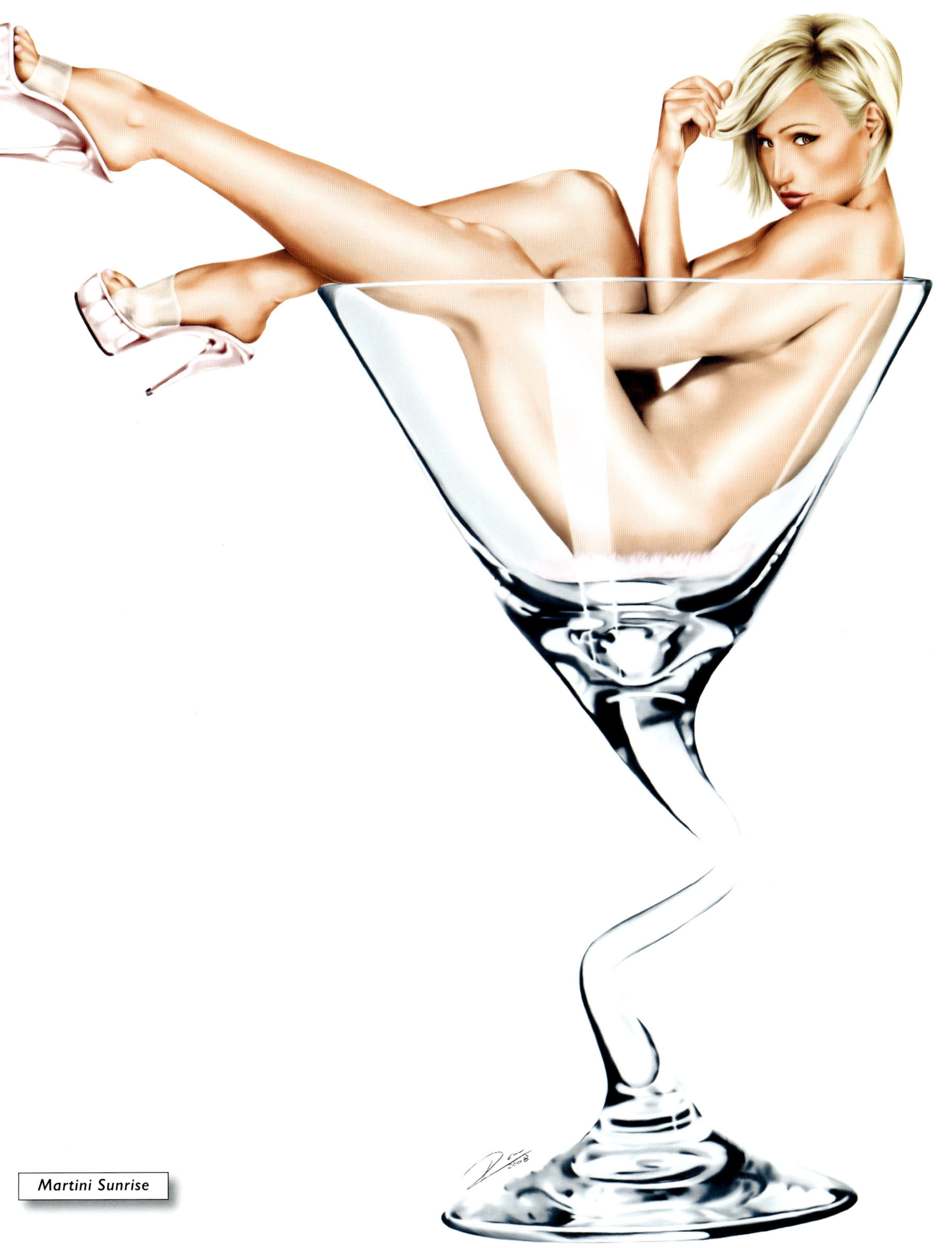

Martini Sunrise

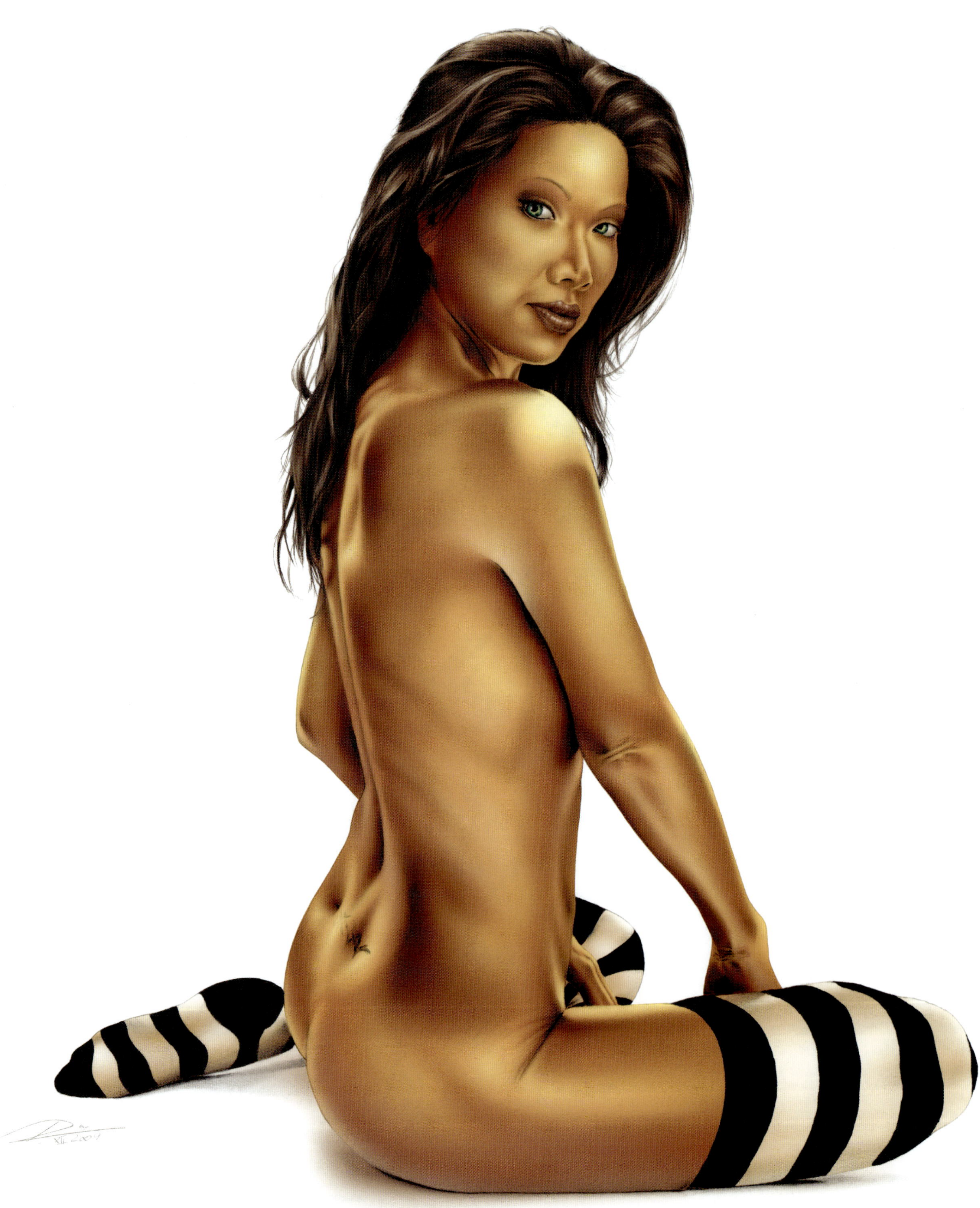

Bella

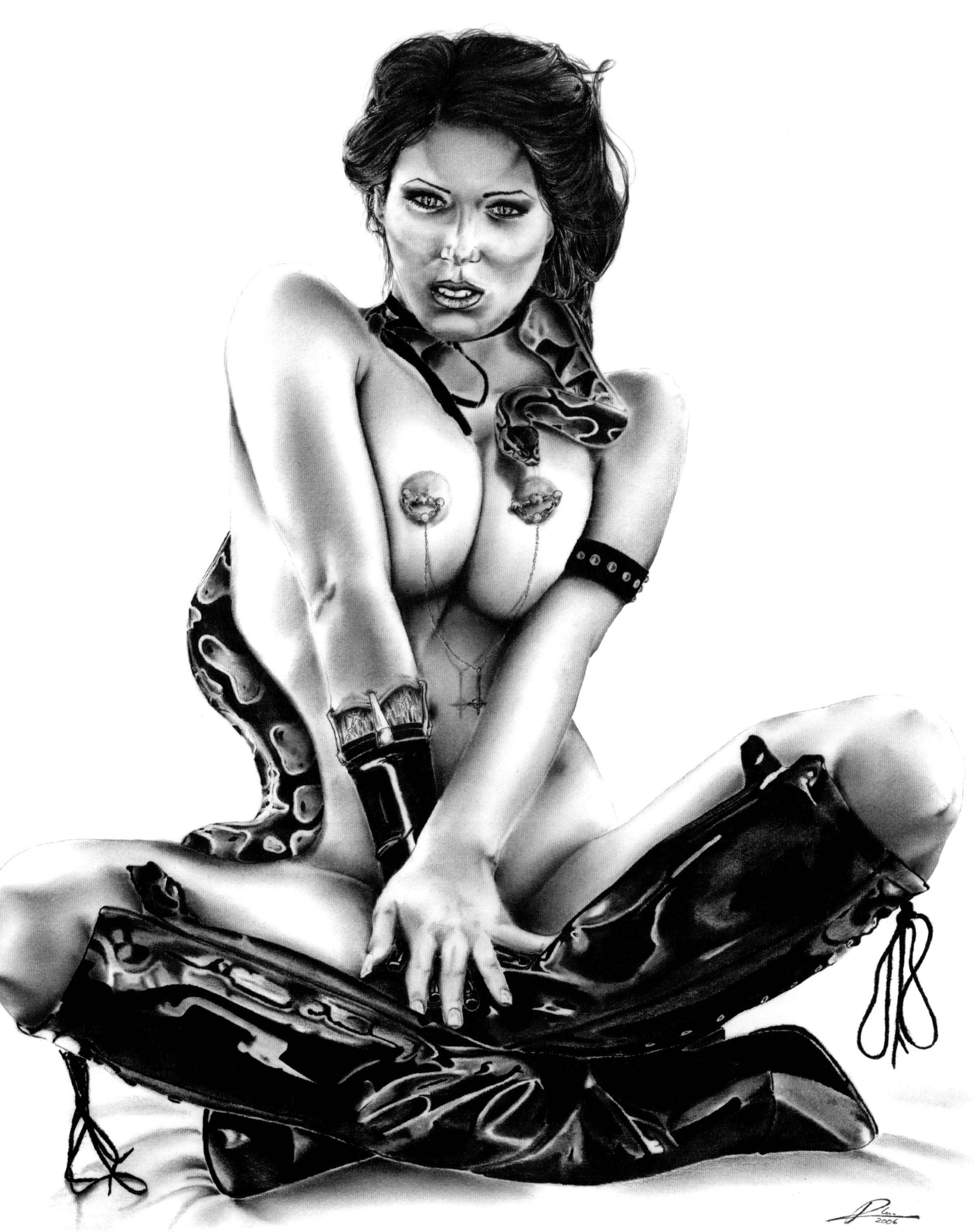

Demonic Beauty

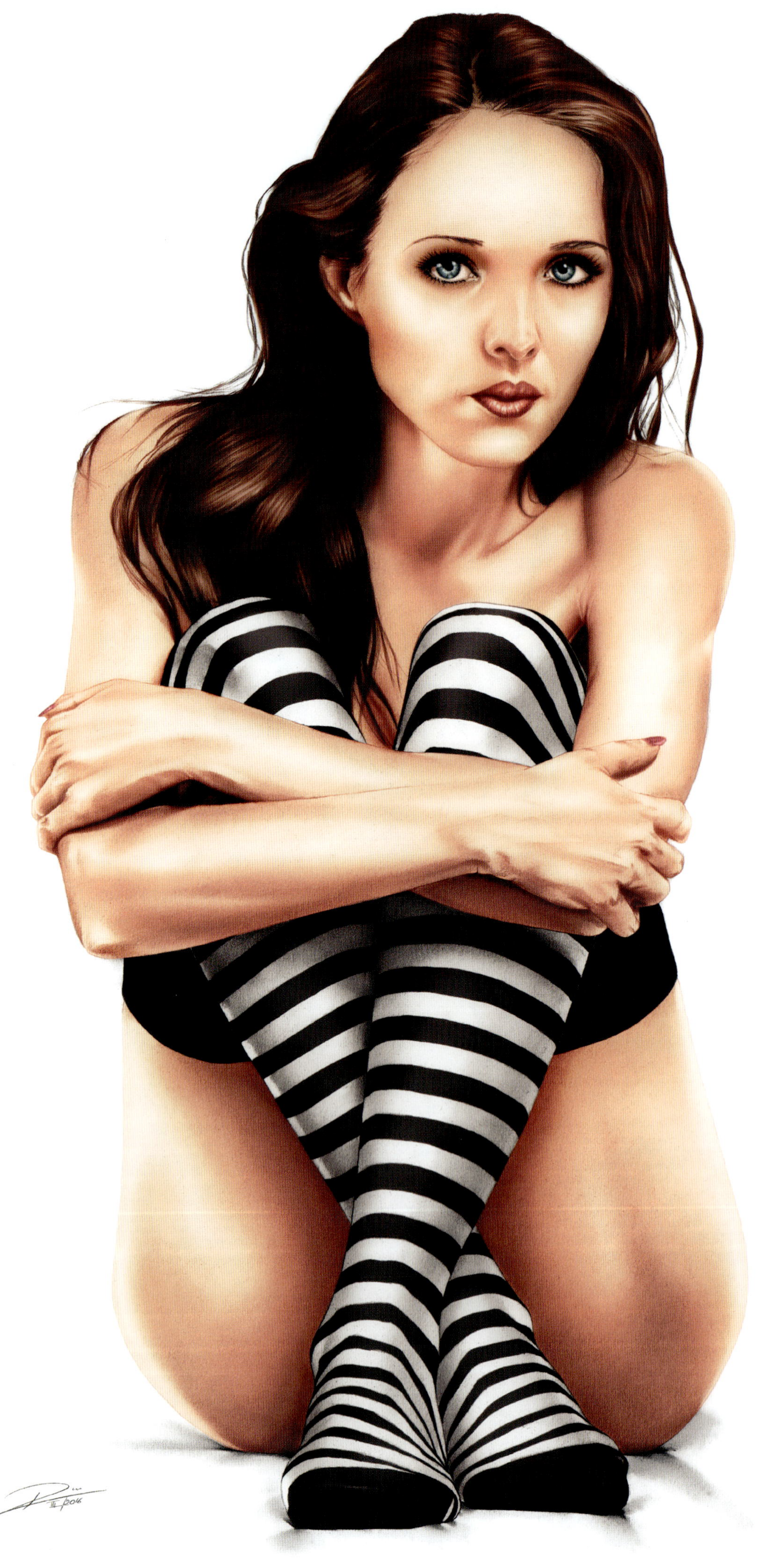

Joylicious

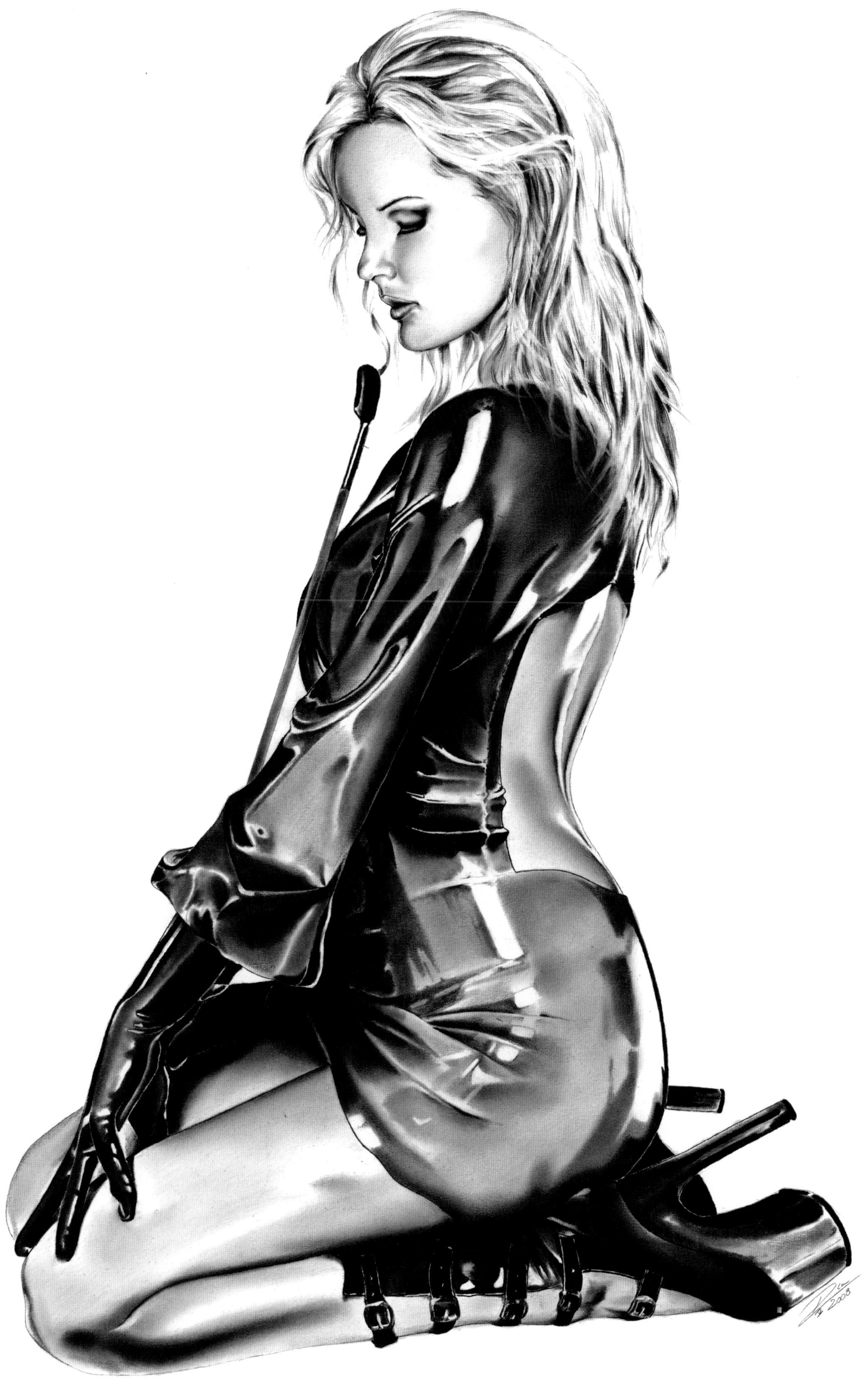

Be Nice

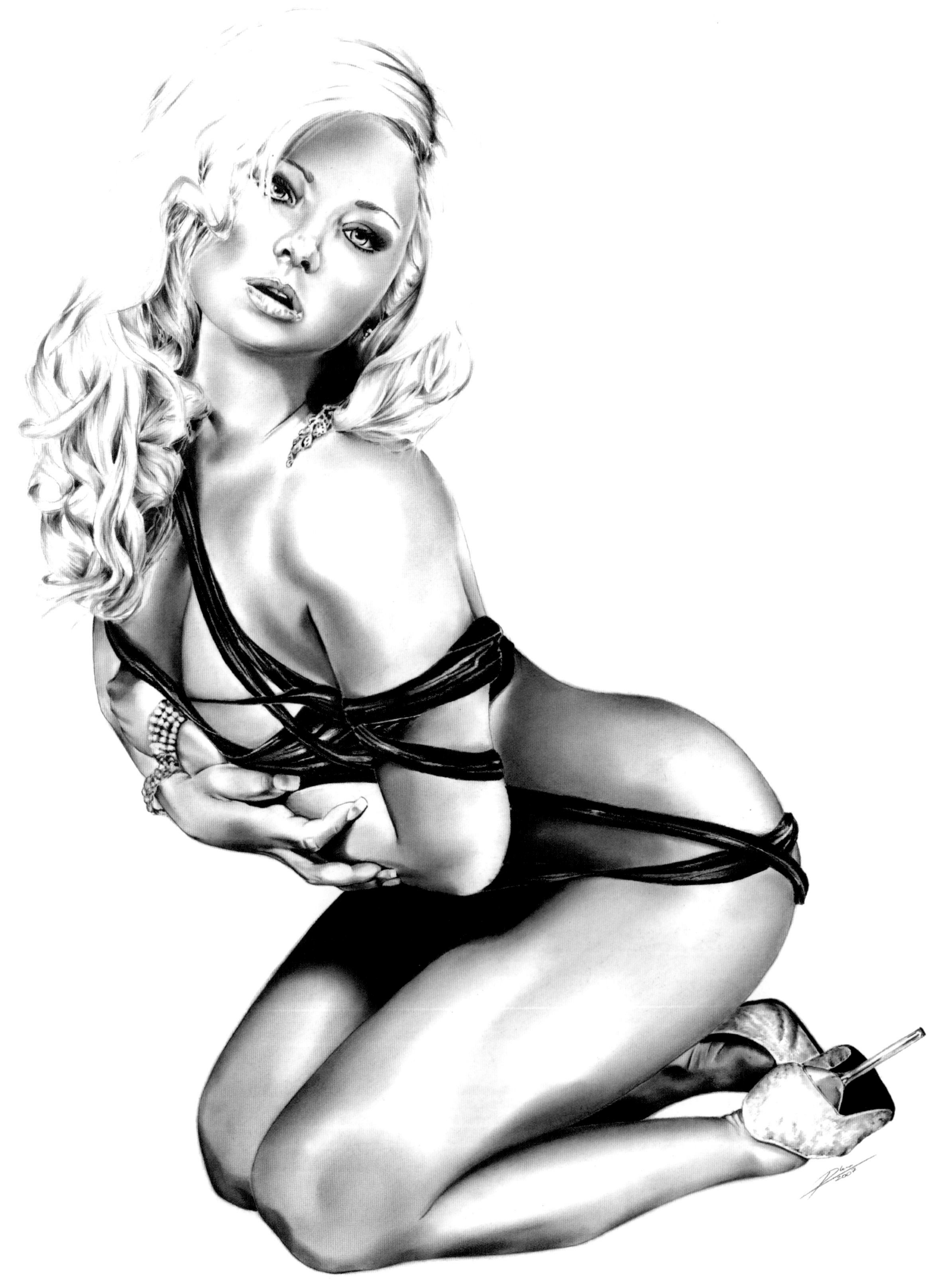

Tied Up

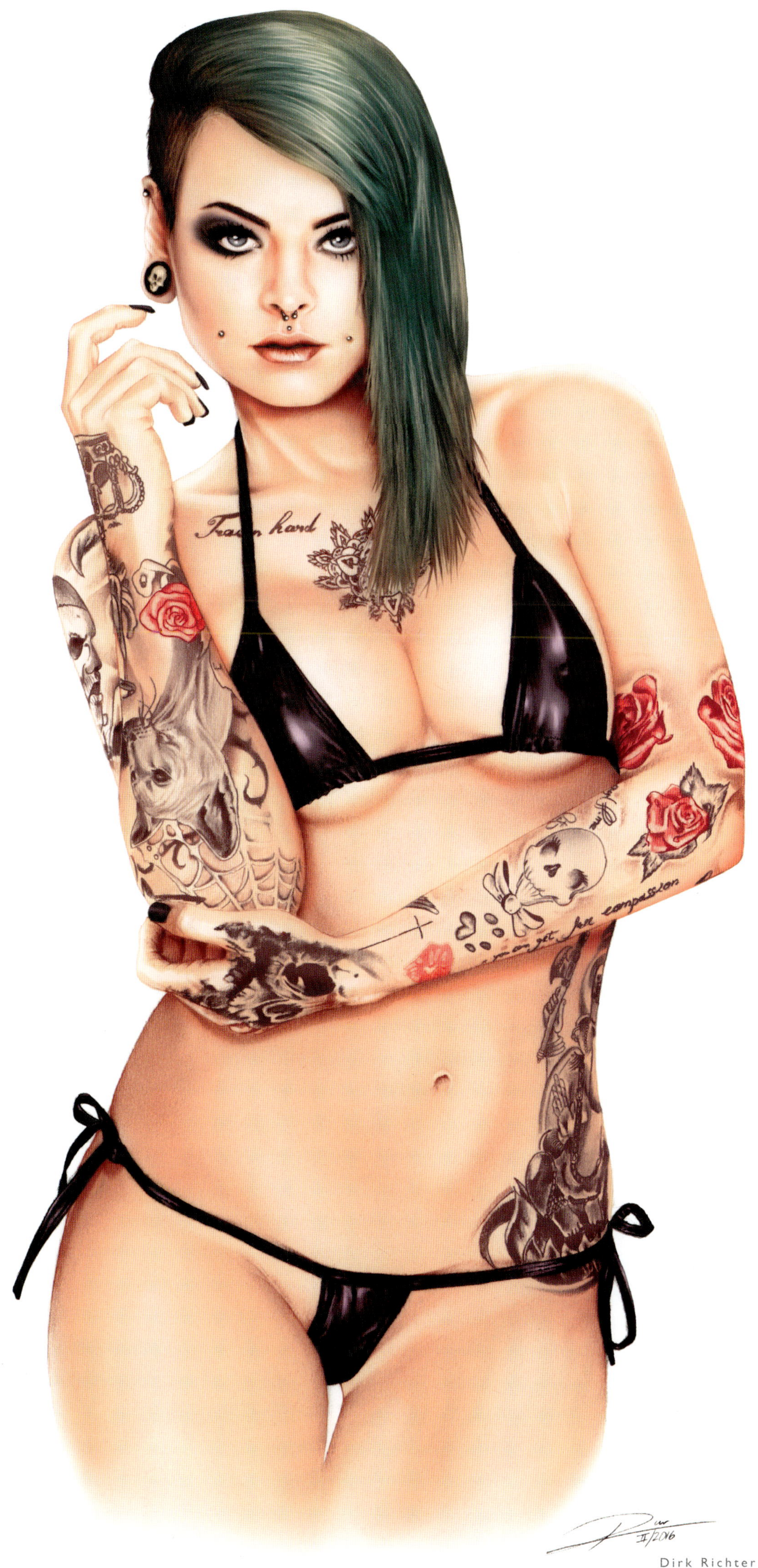

So What?

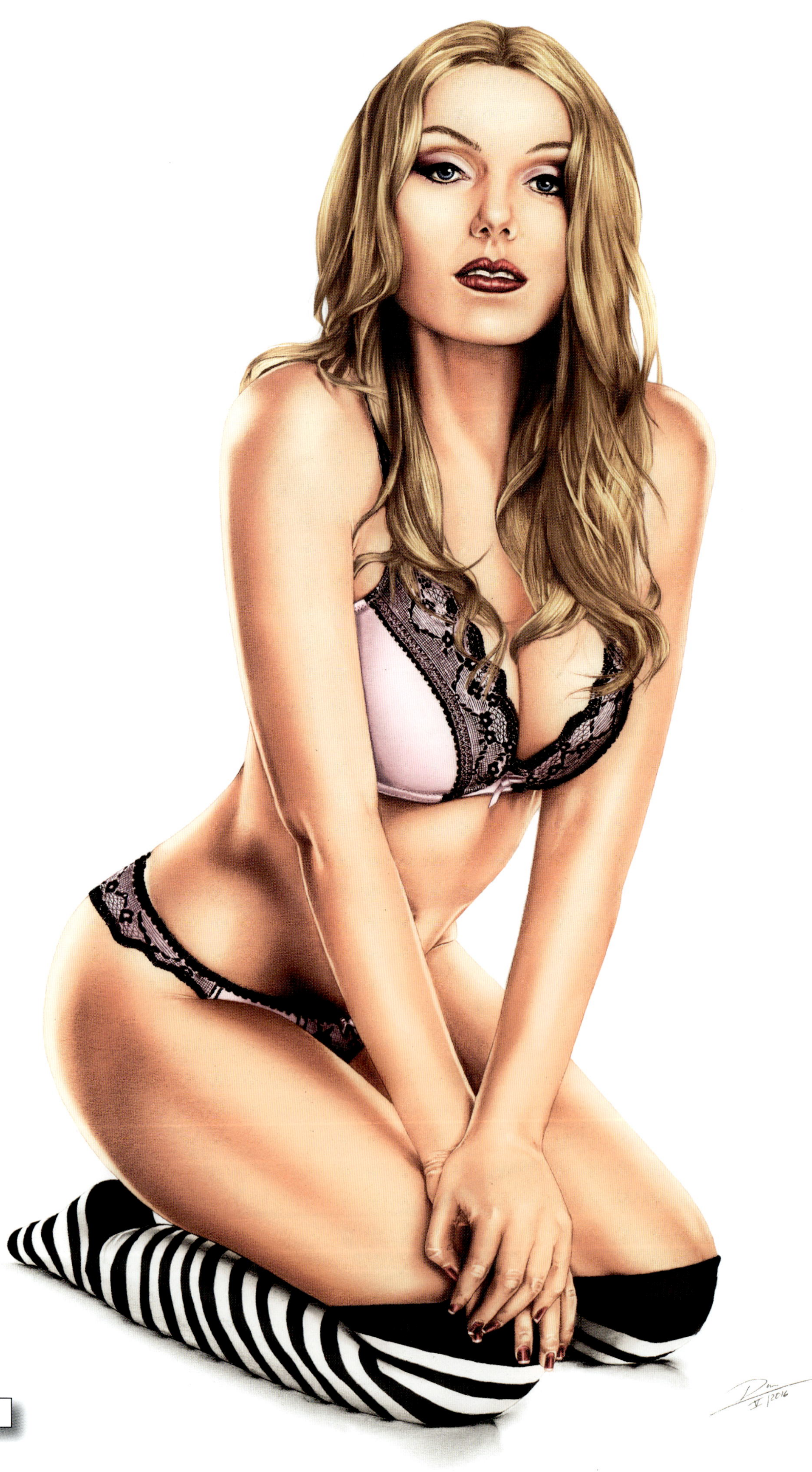

Grace

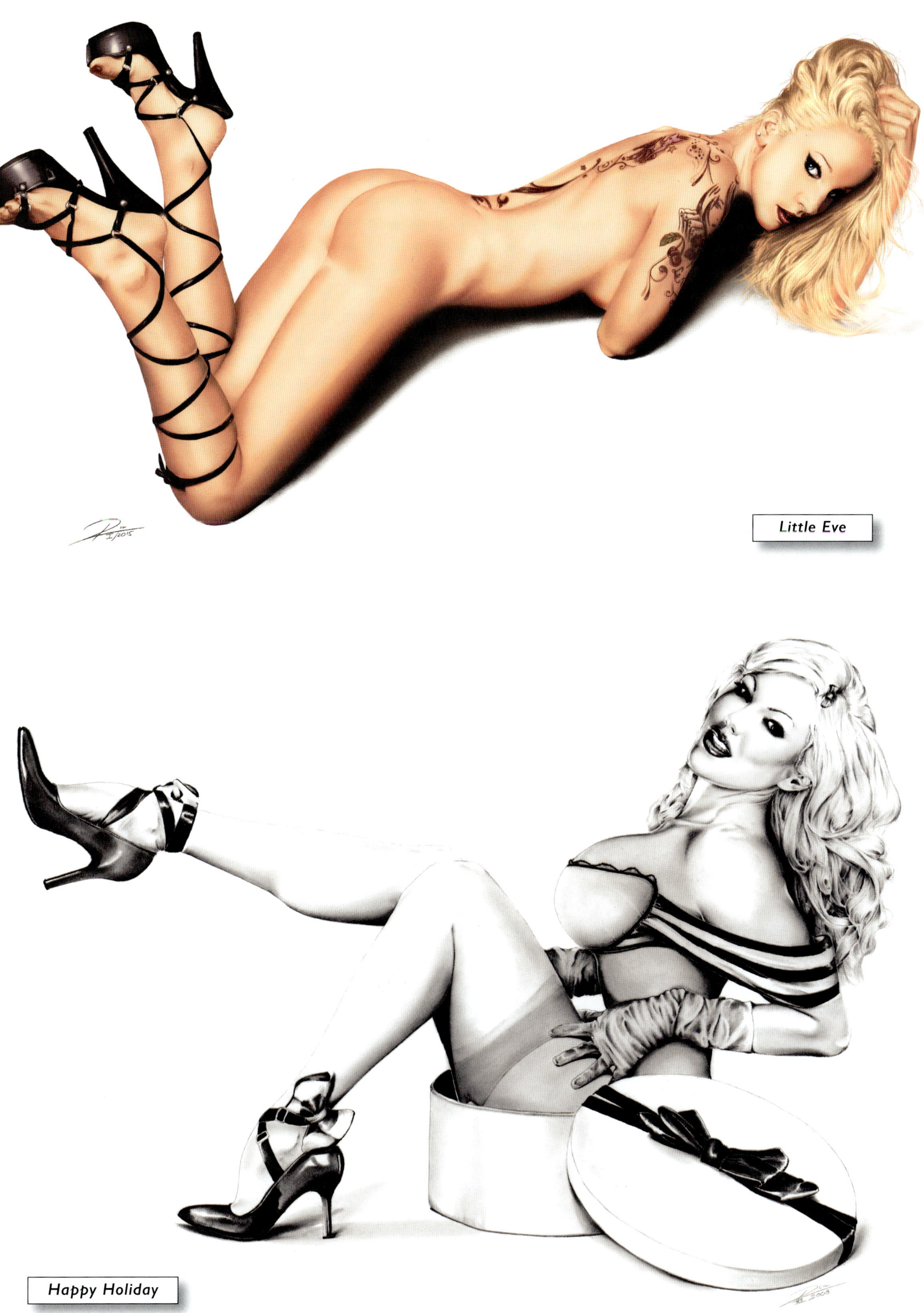

Little Eve

Happy Holiday

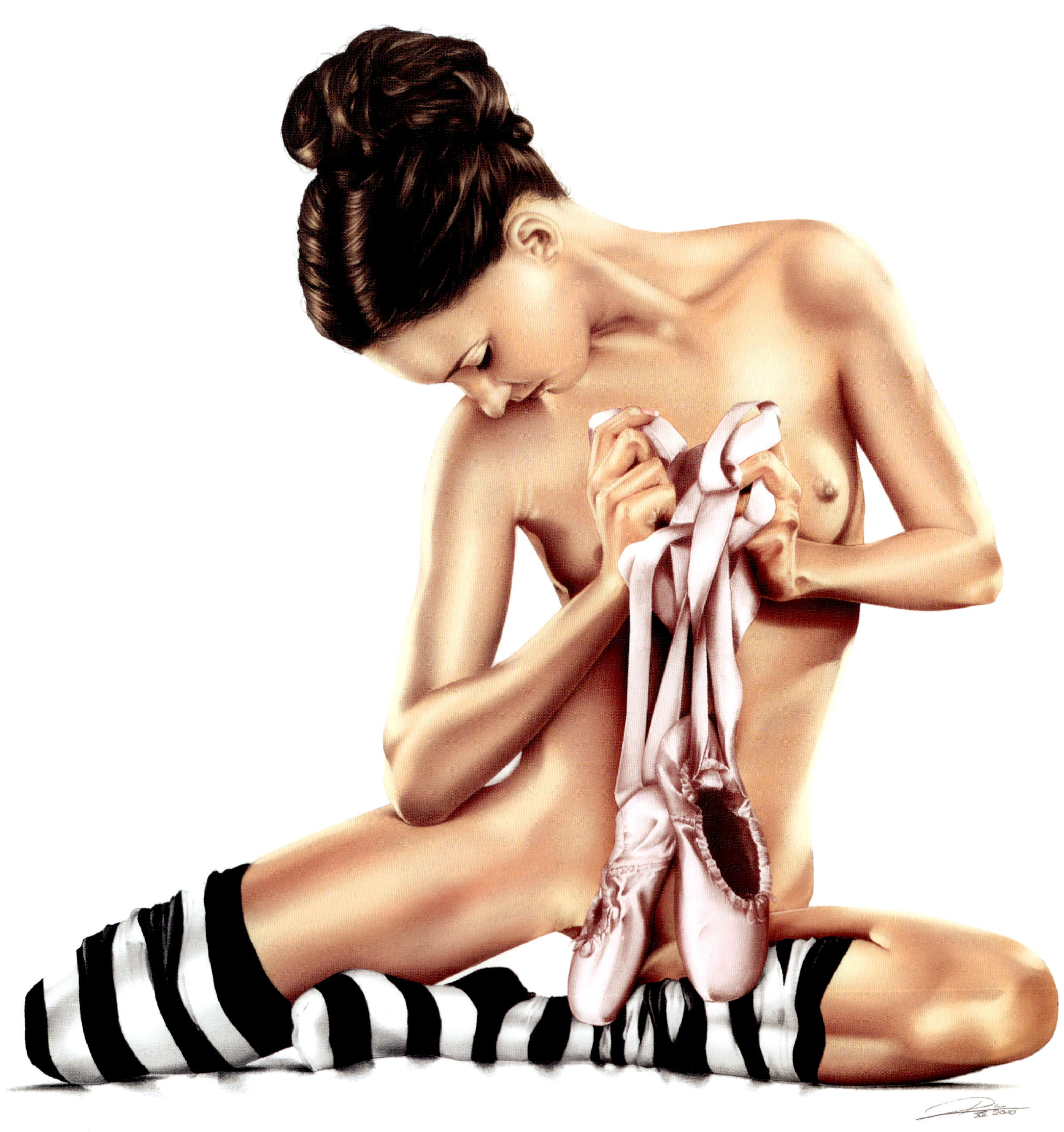

Ballerina

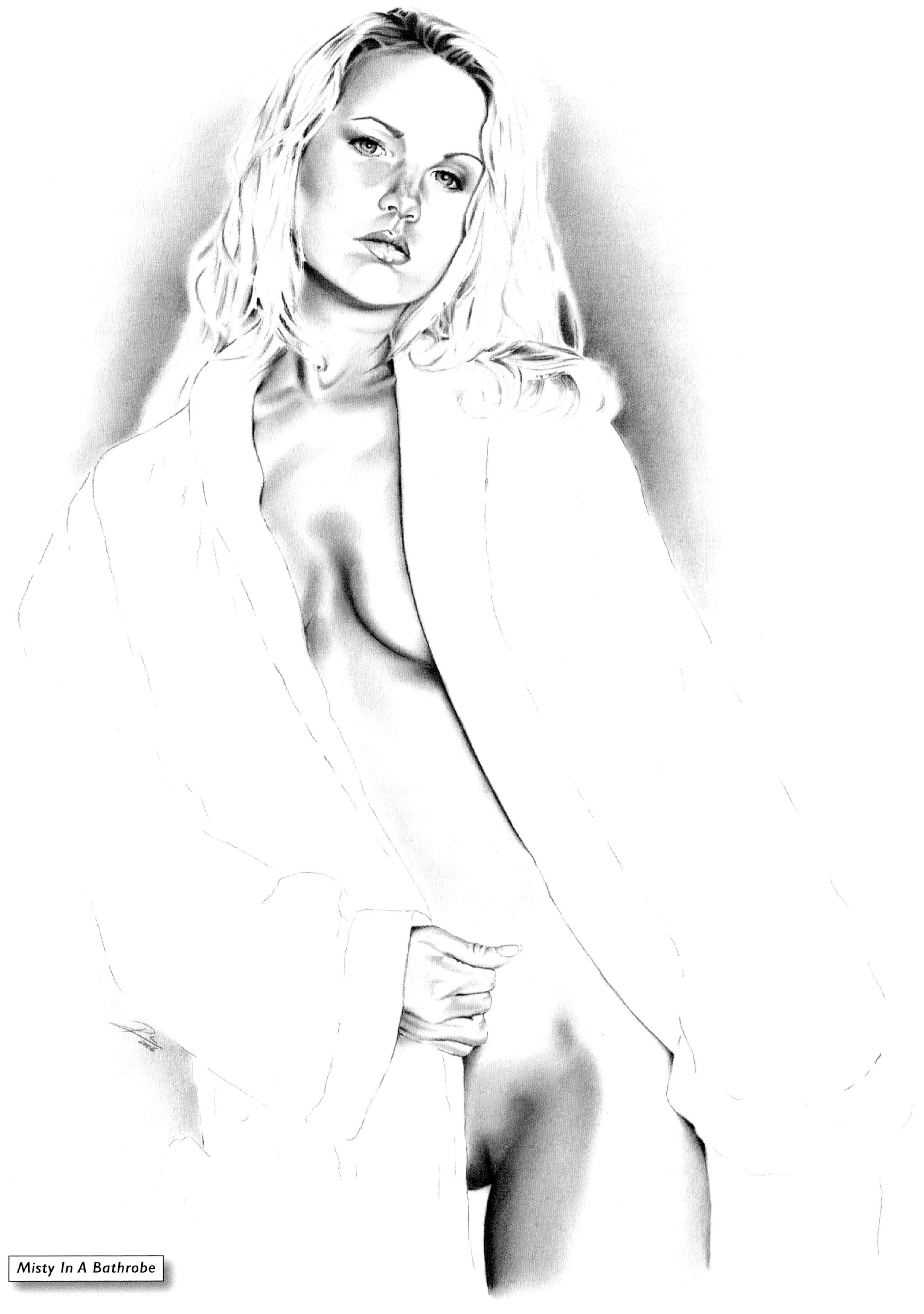

Misty In A Bathrobe

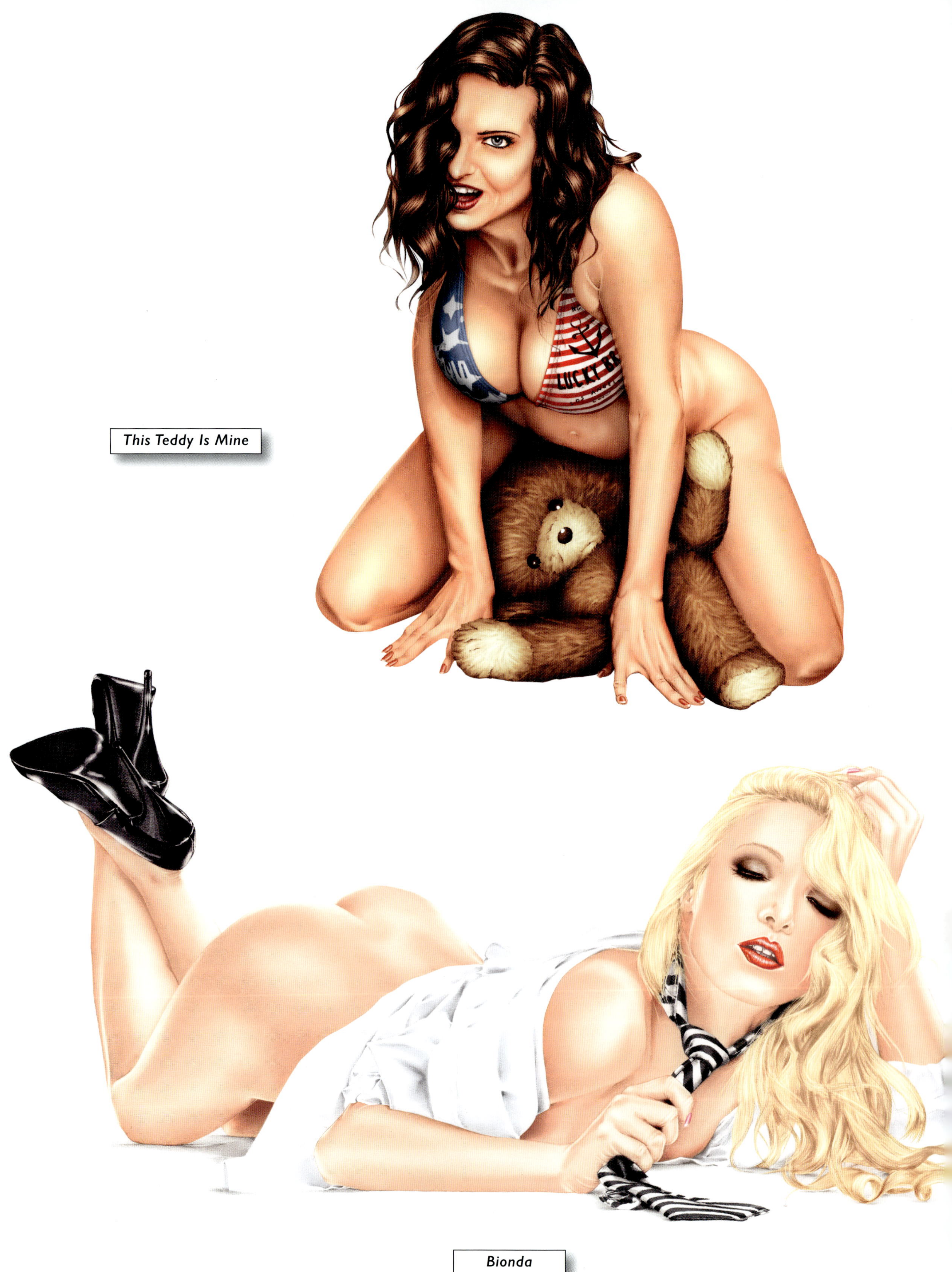

This Teddy Is Mine

Bionda

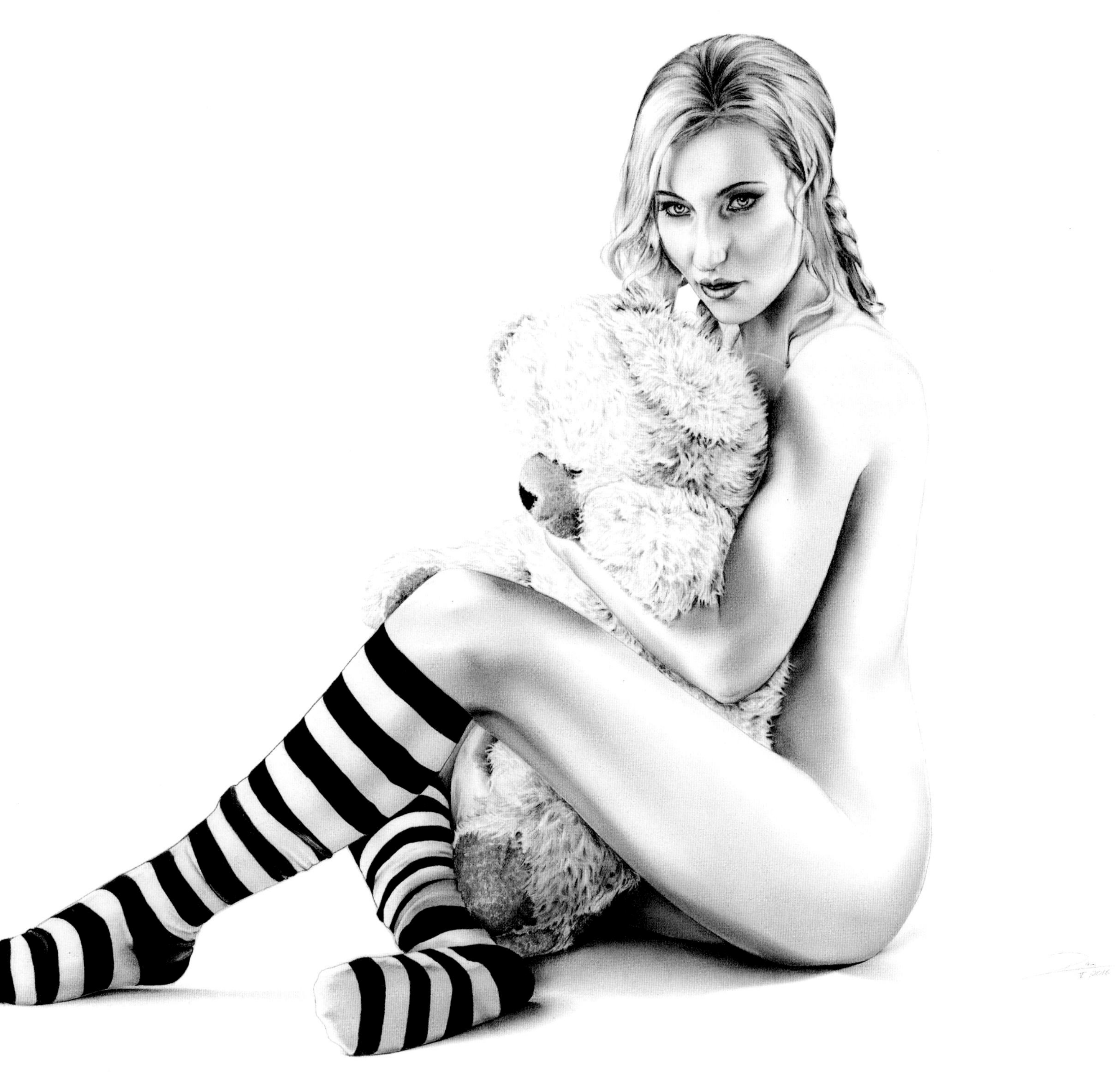

Cuddle Me

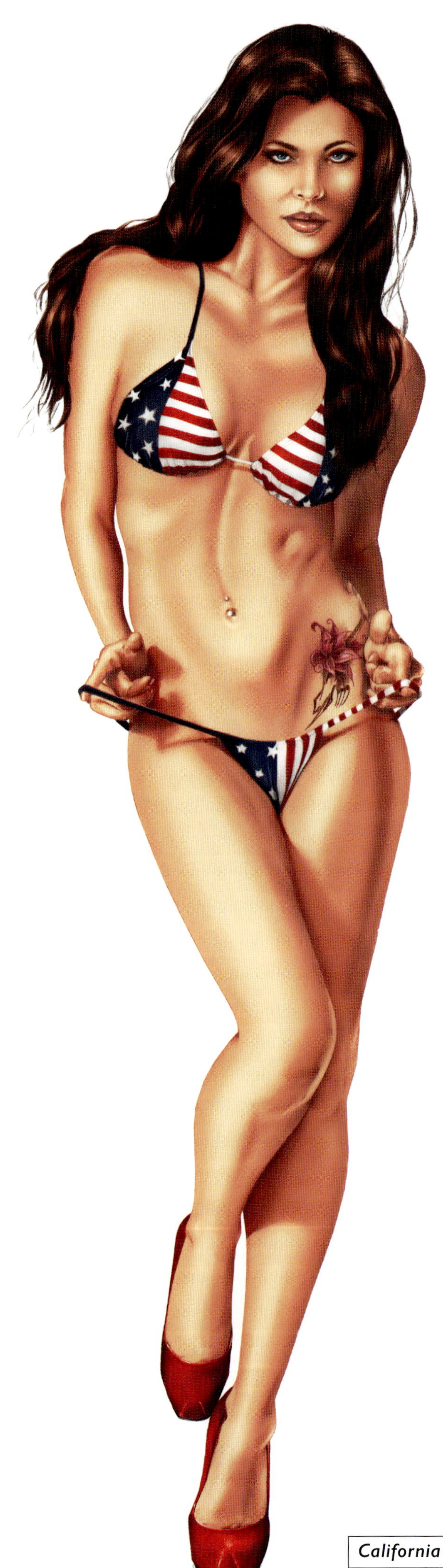

California Girl

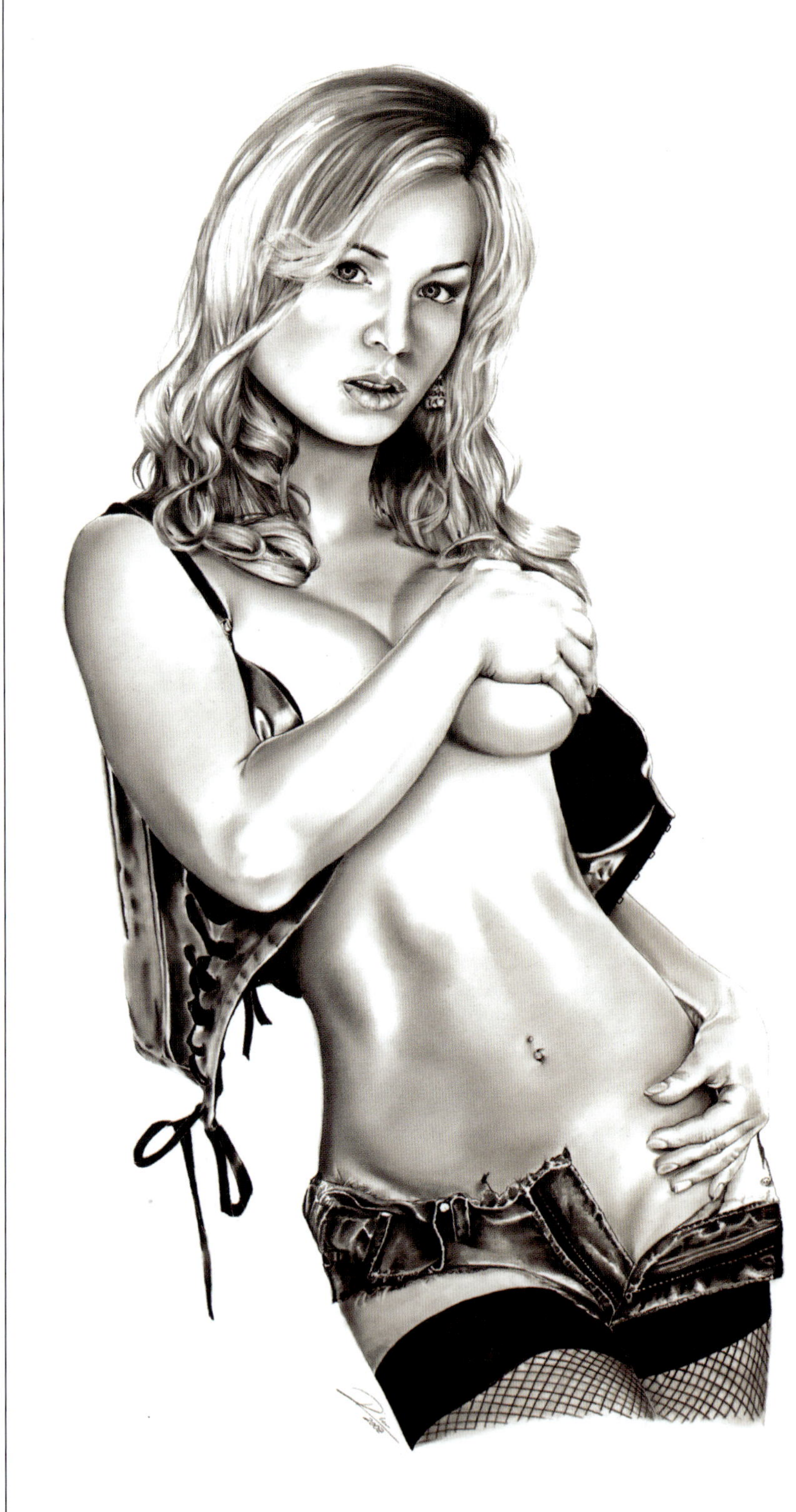

Don't Peek

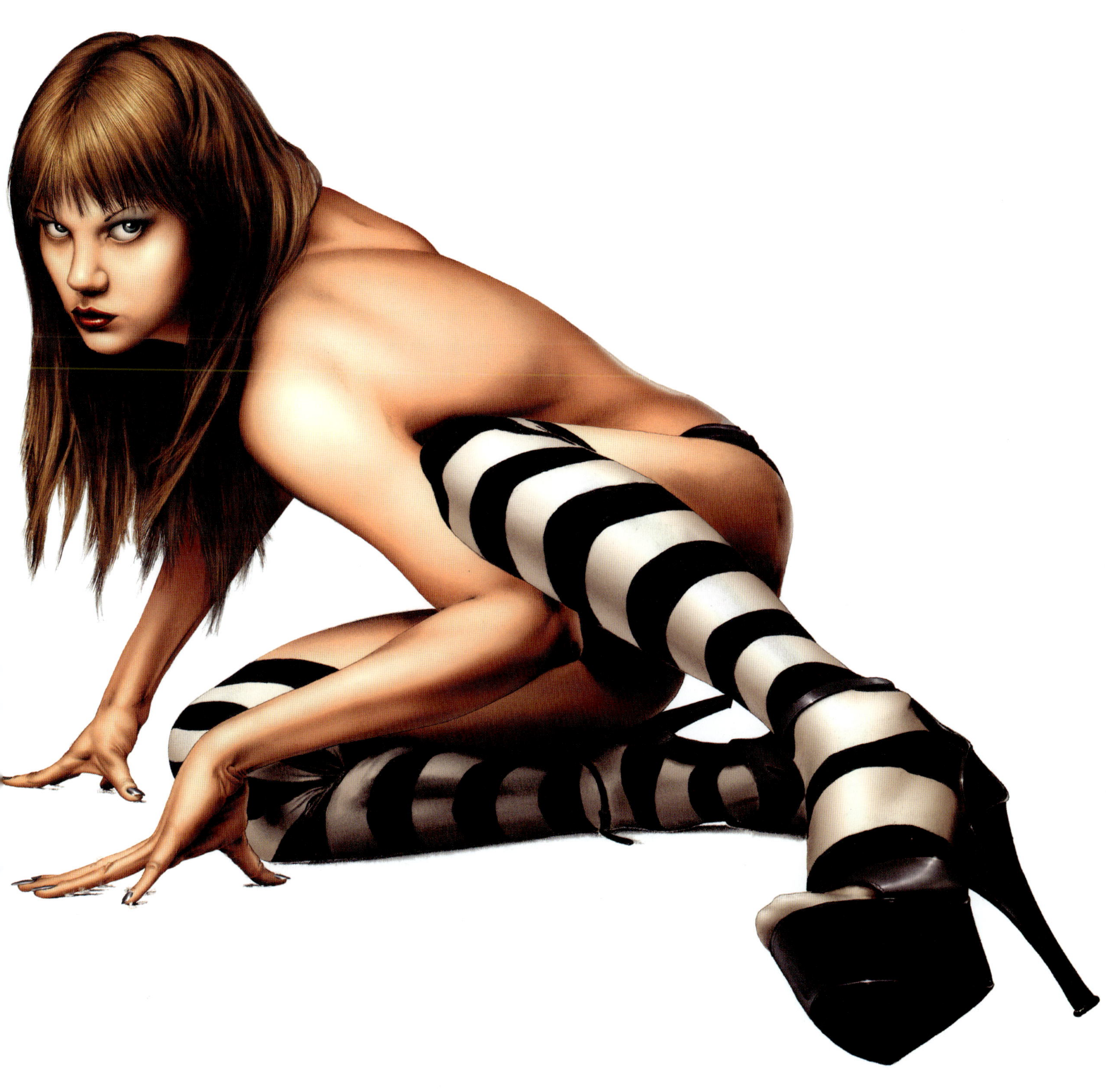

Katzz

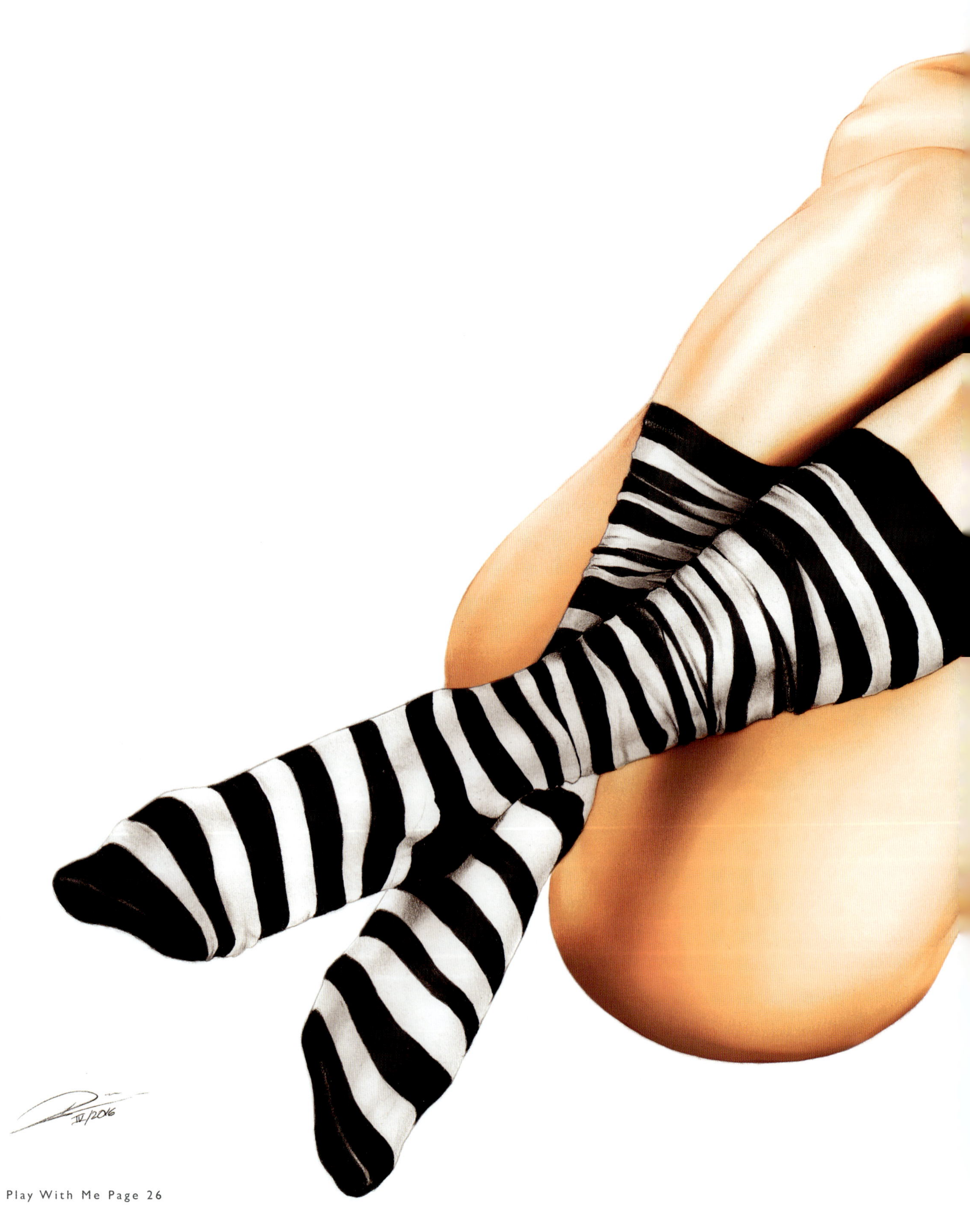

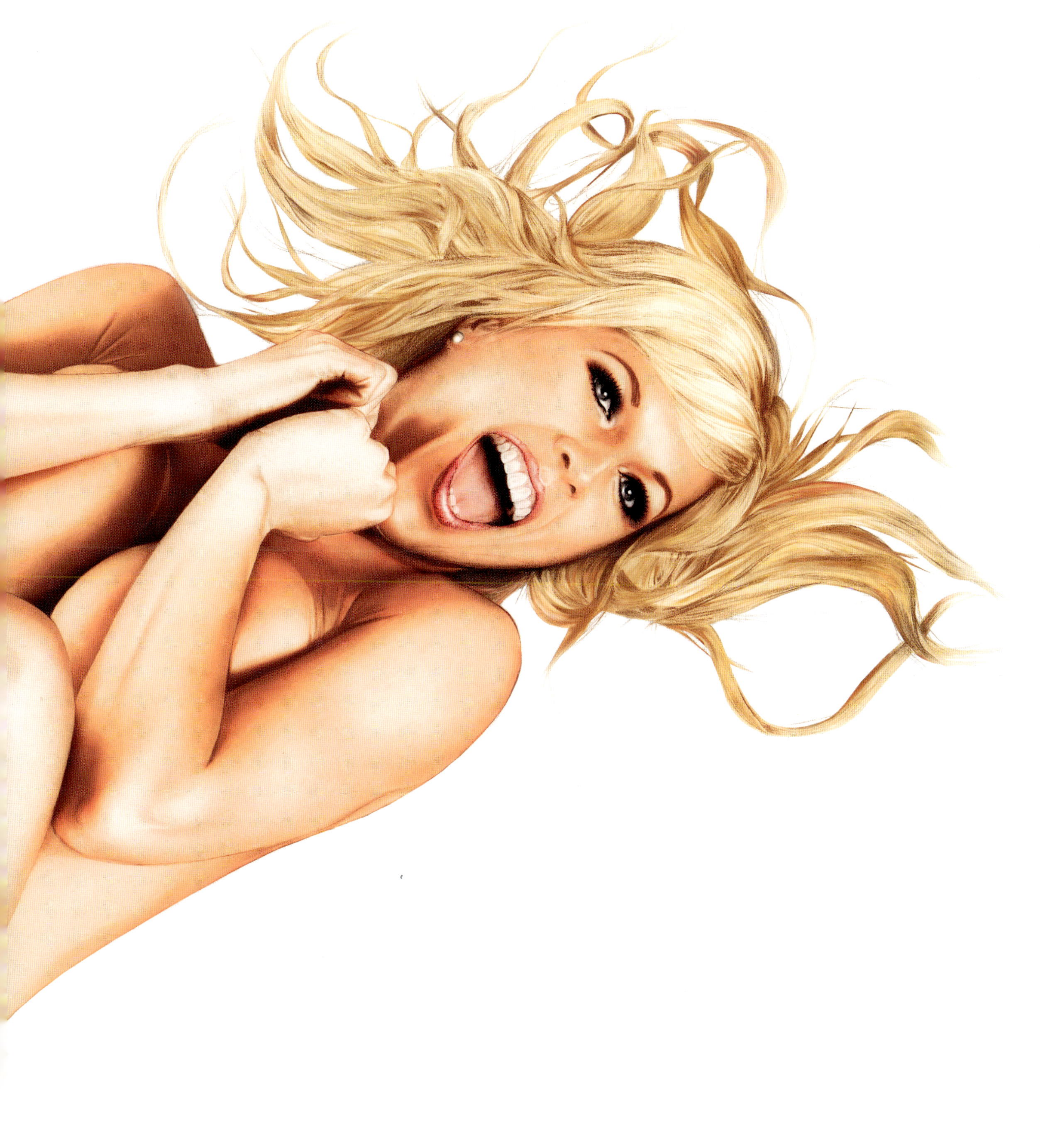

Play With Me

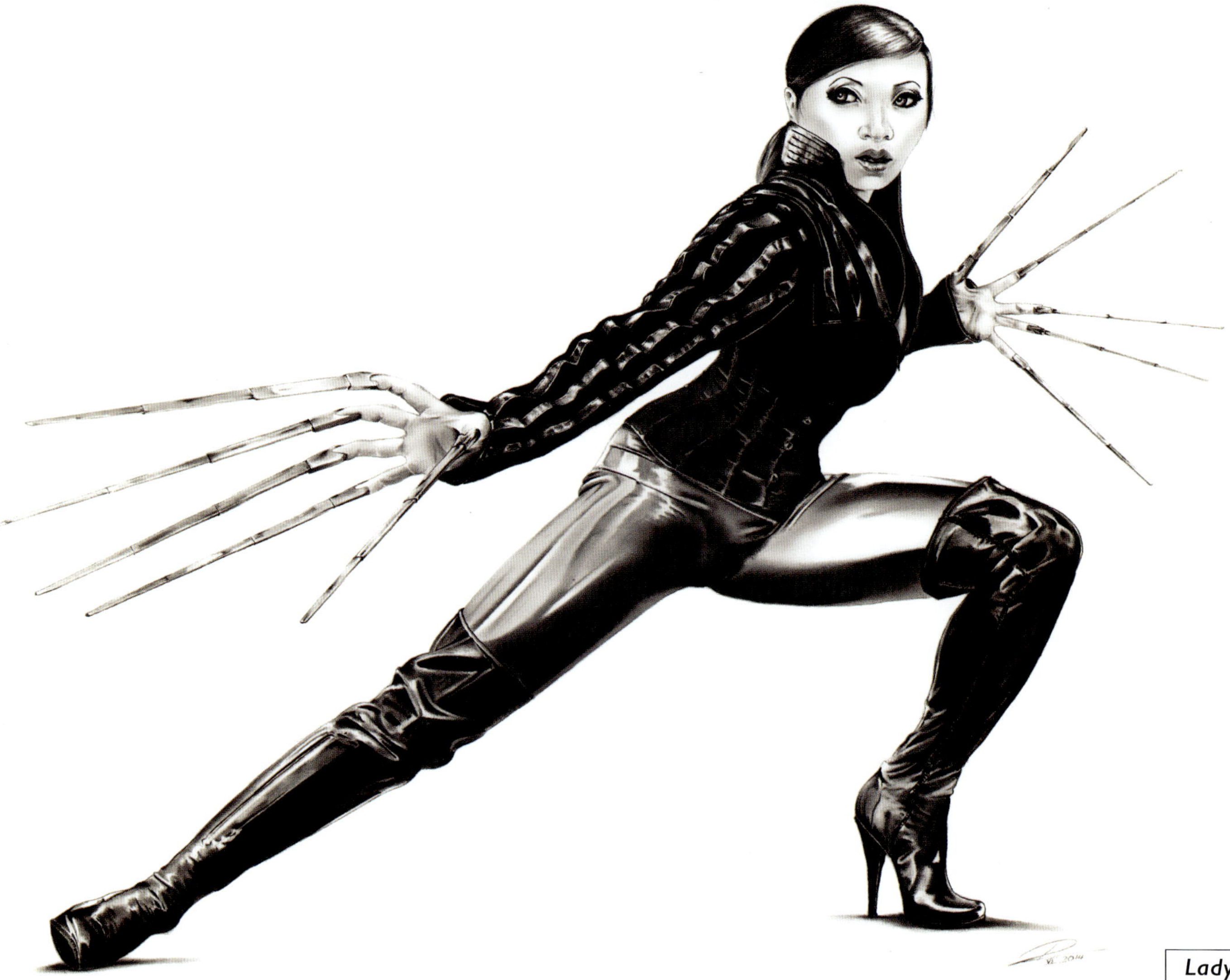

Lady Deathstrik

Rey

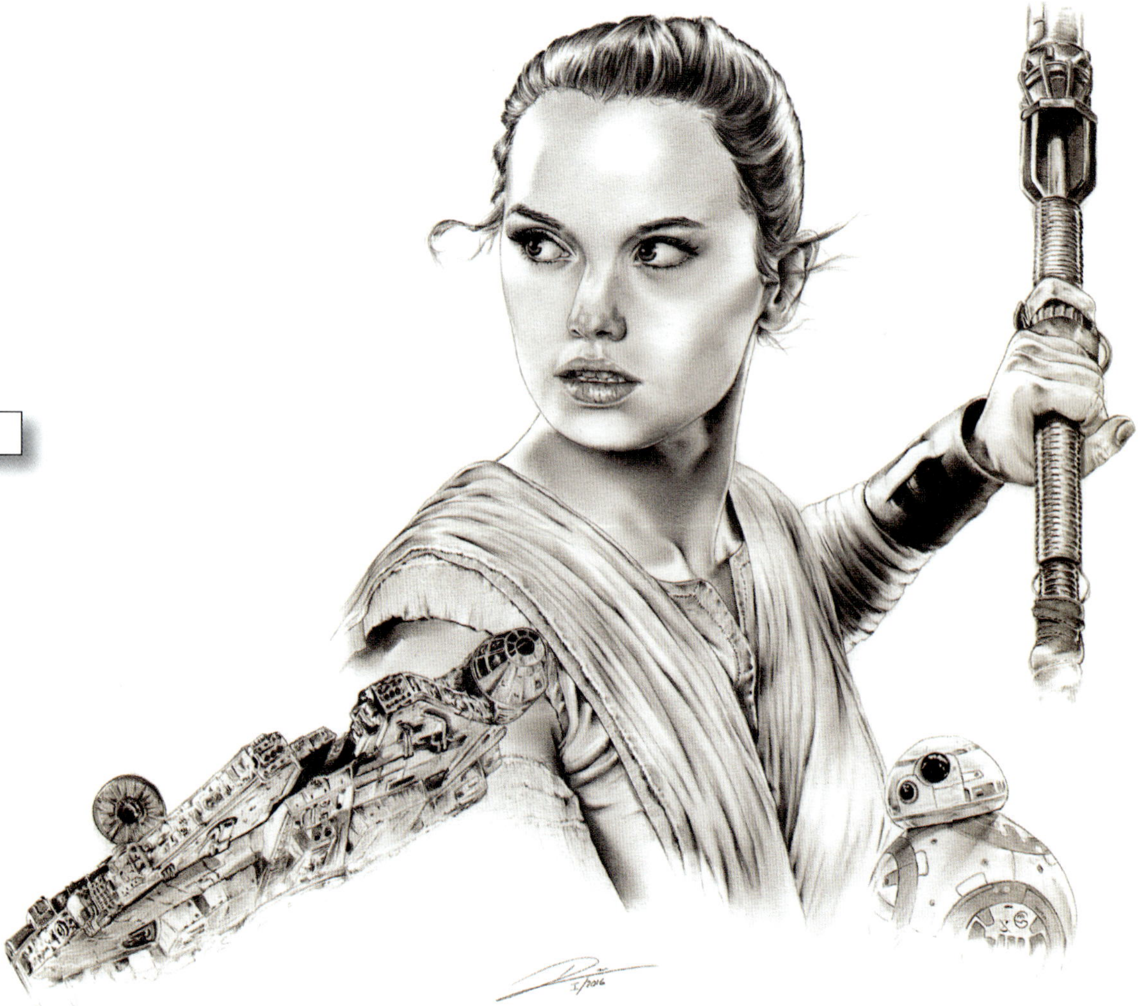

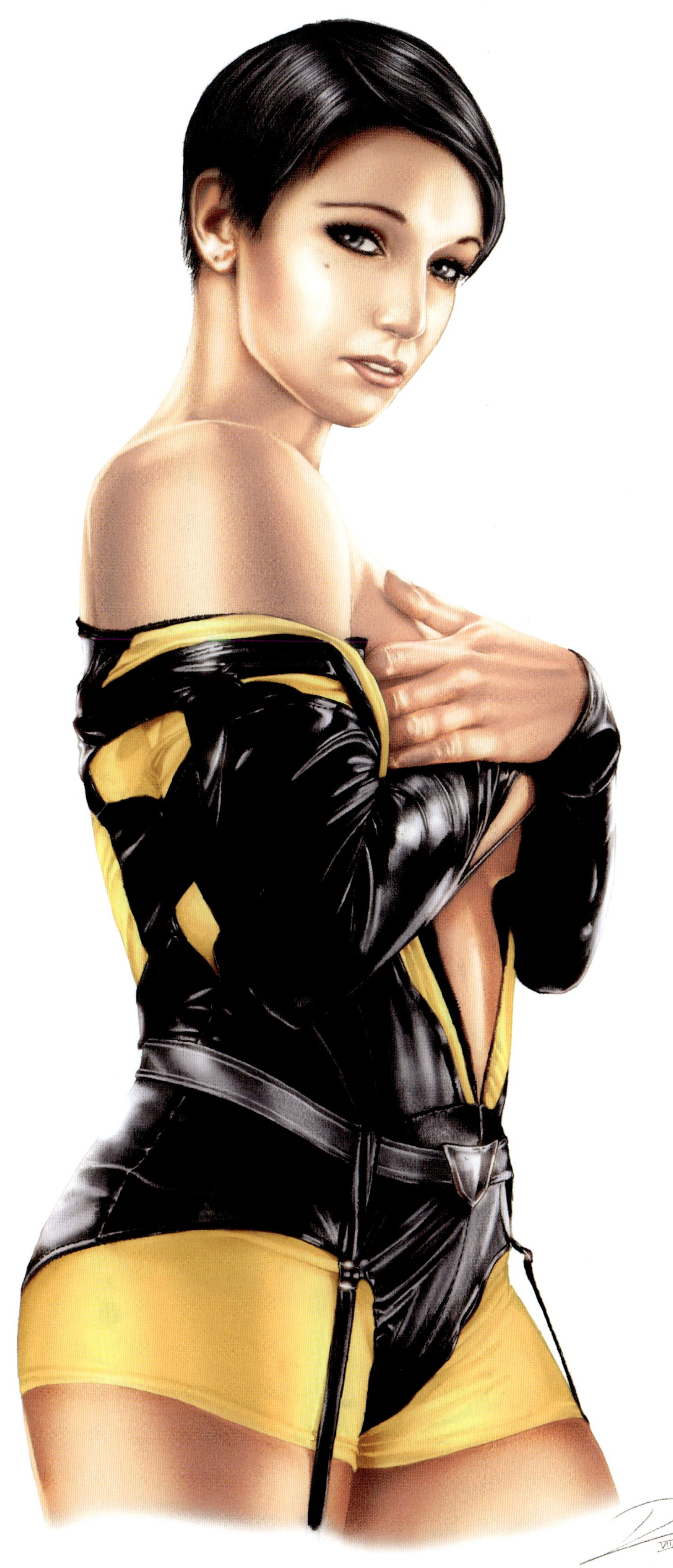

Silk Spectre

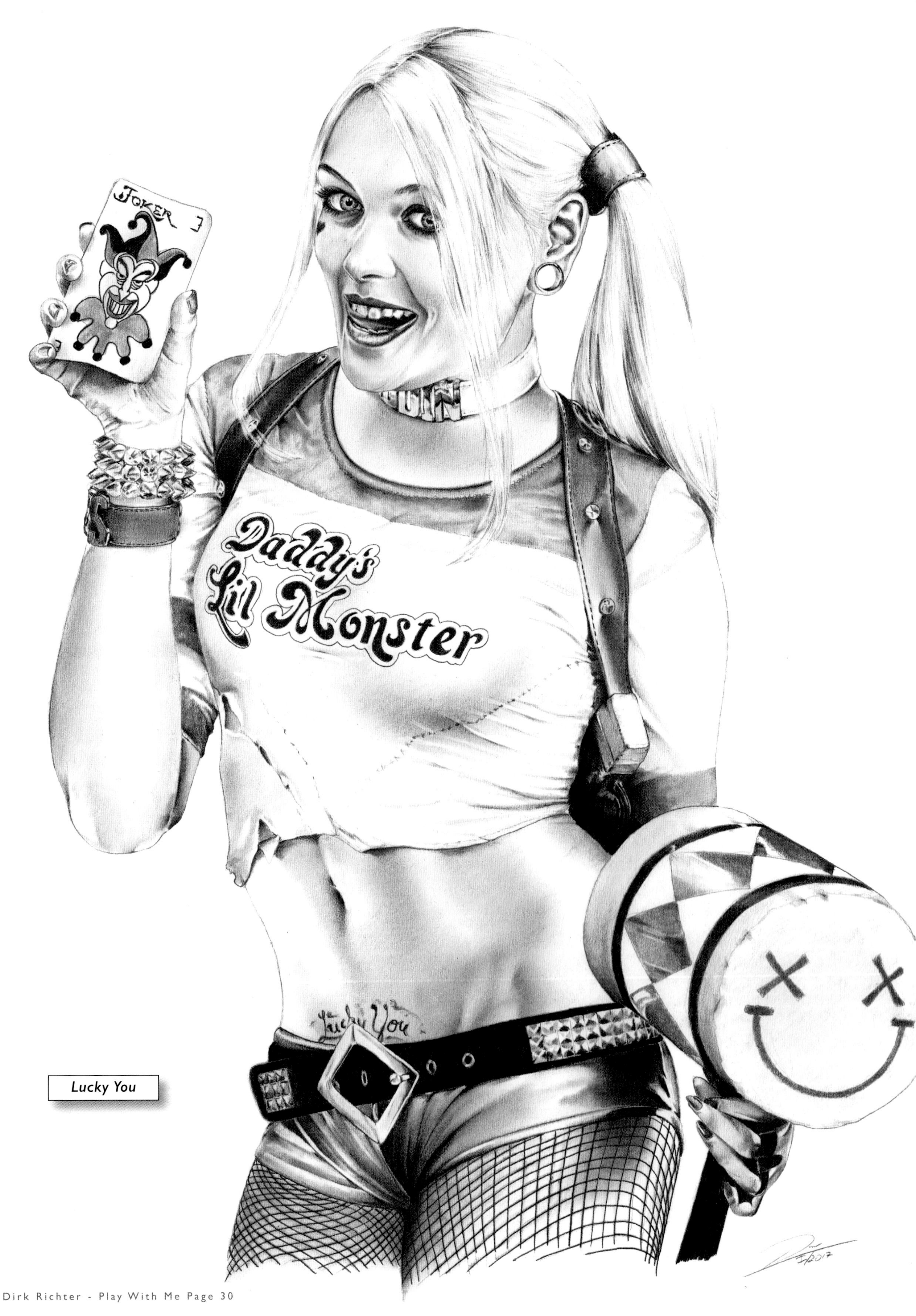

Lucky You

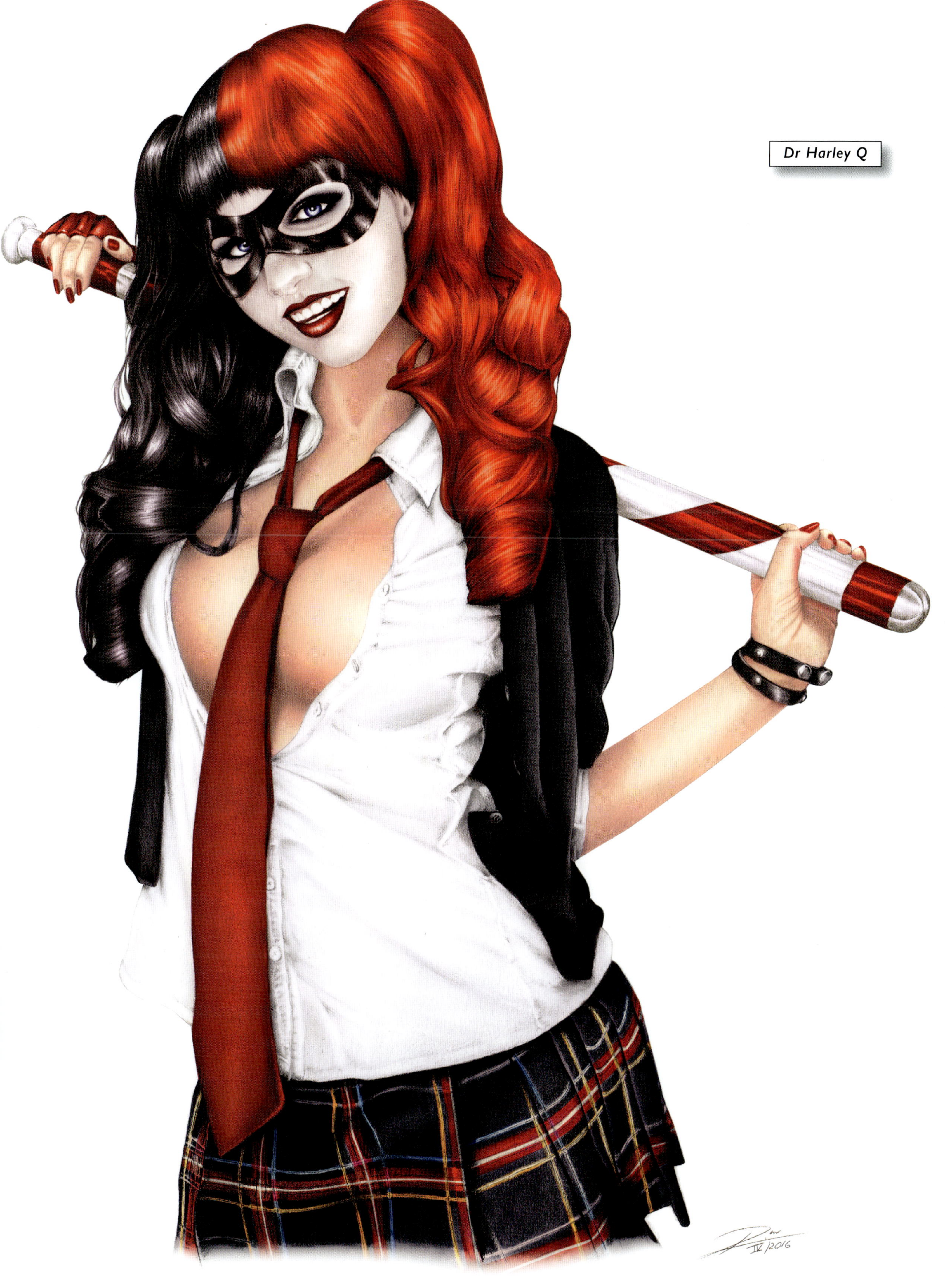
Dr Harley Q

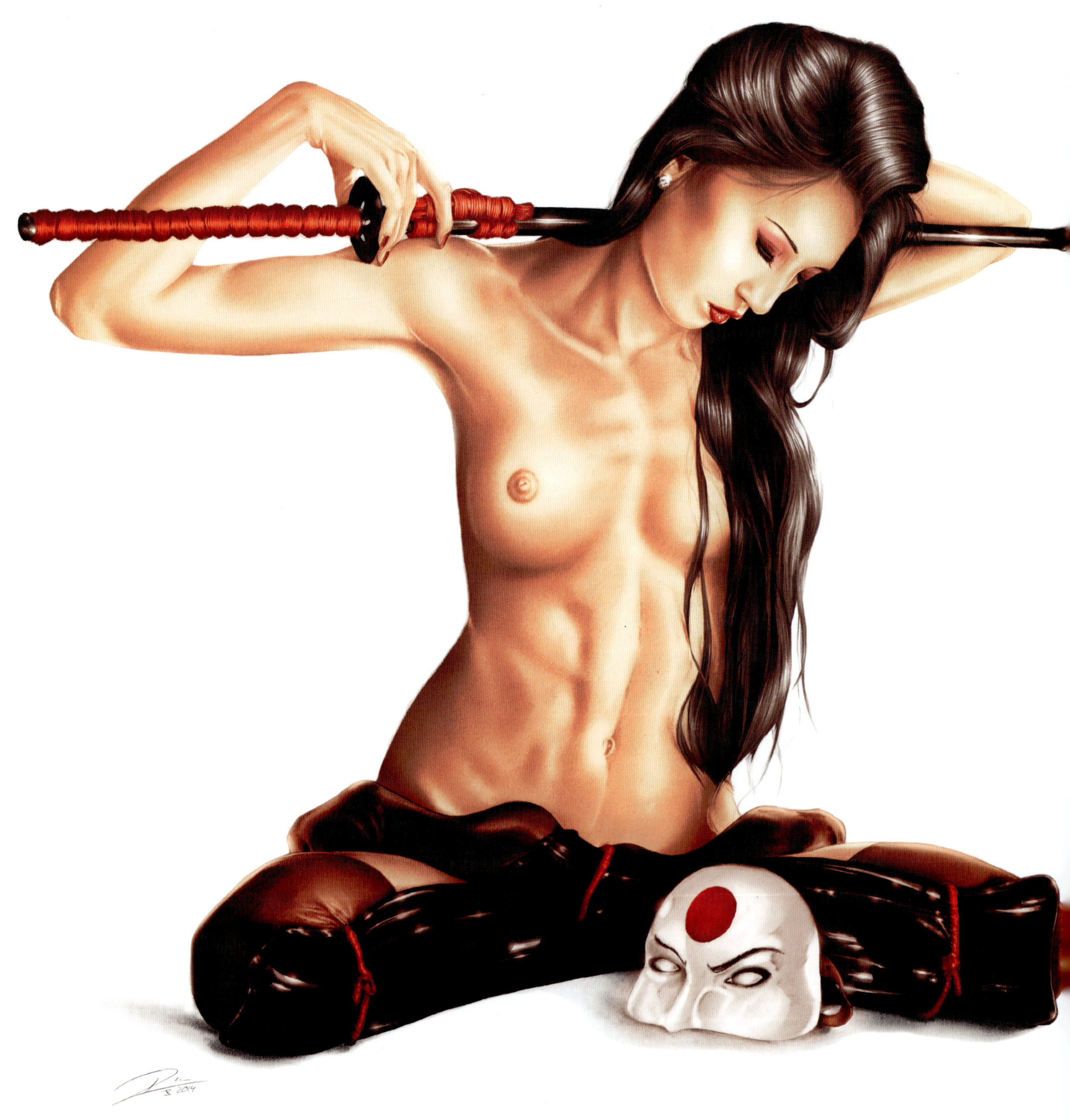

Katana

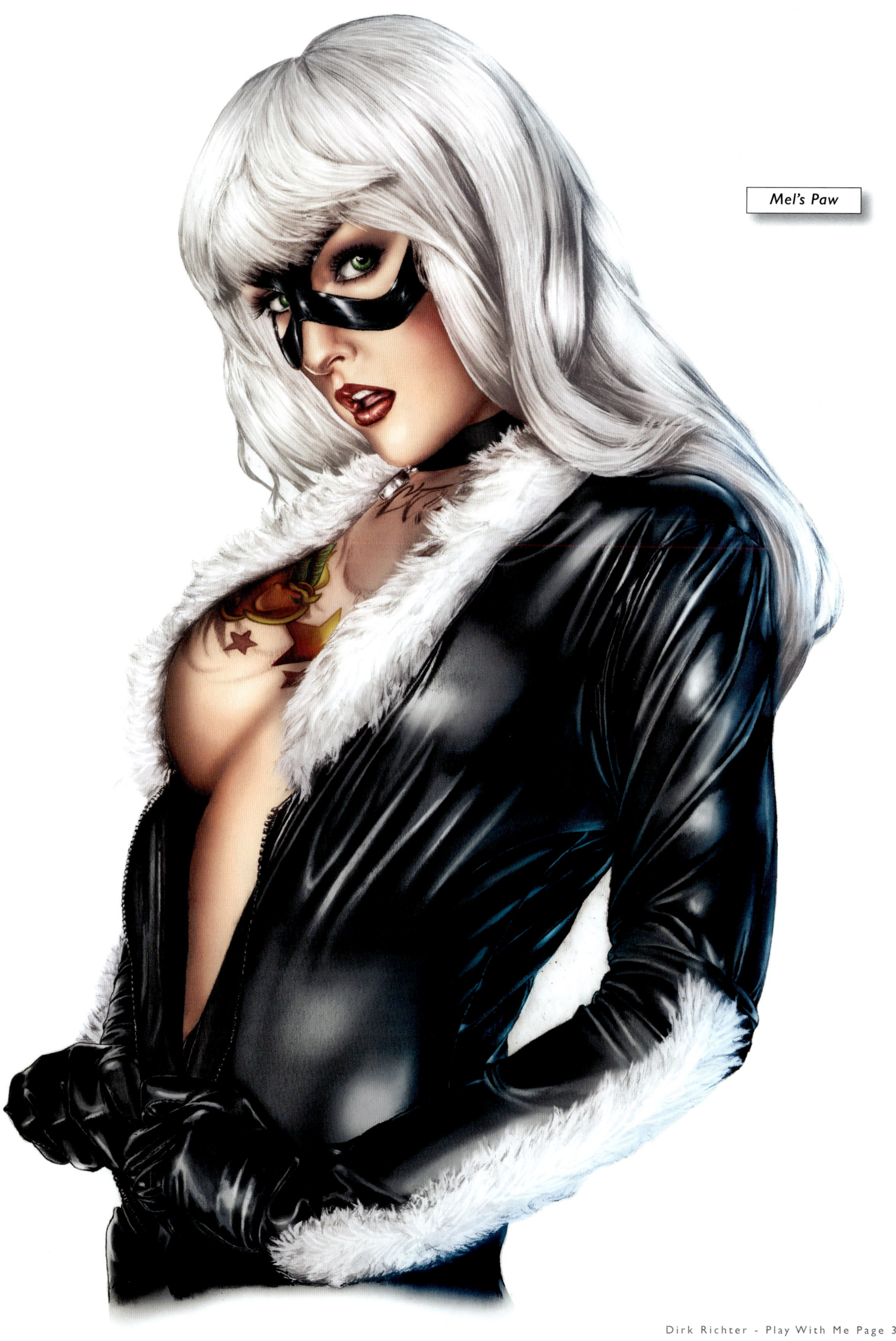

Mel's Paw

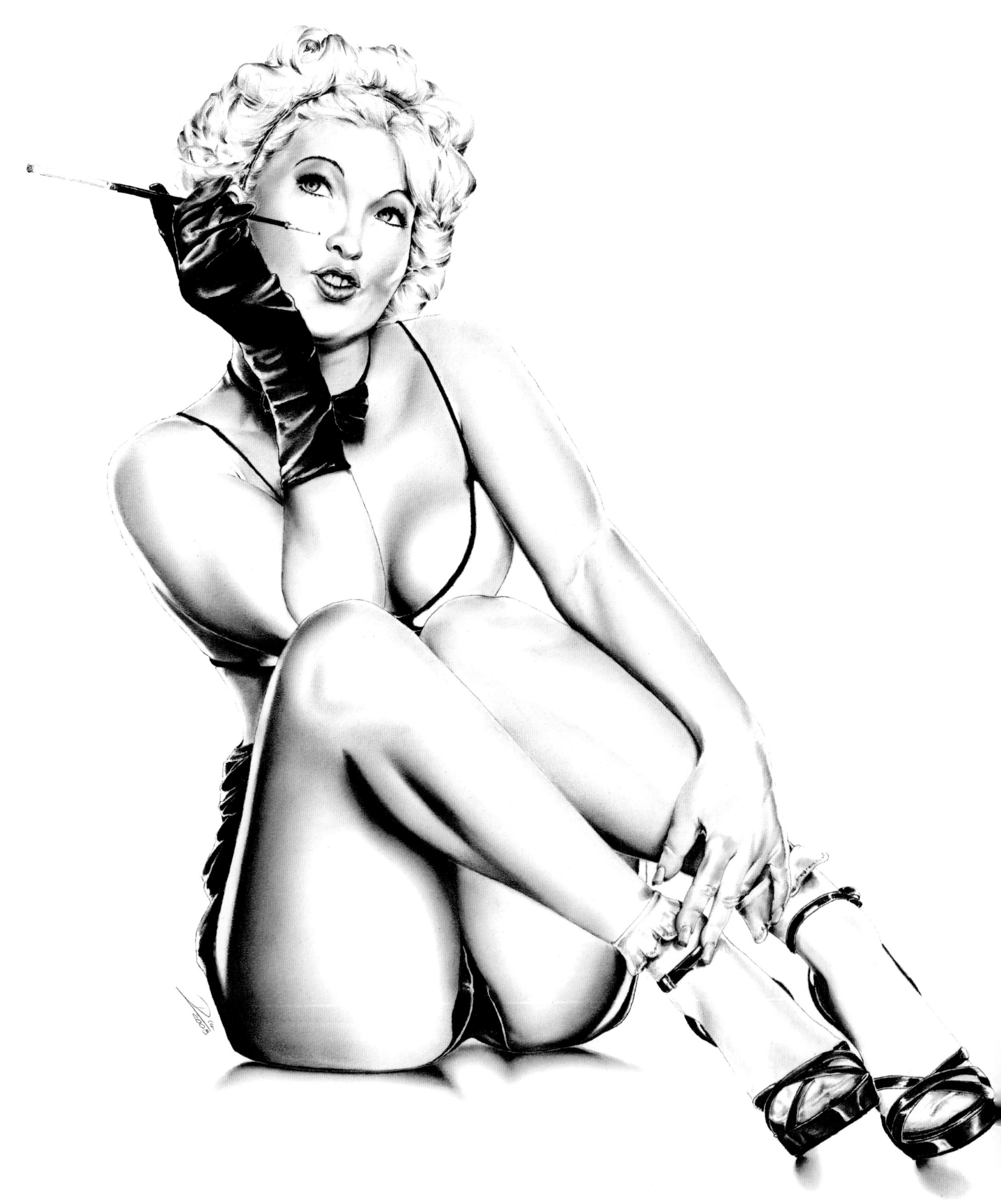

Hollywood Glamour

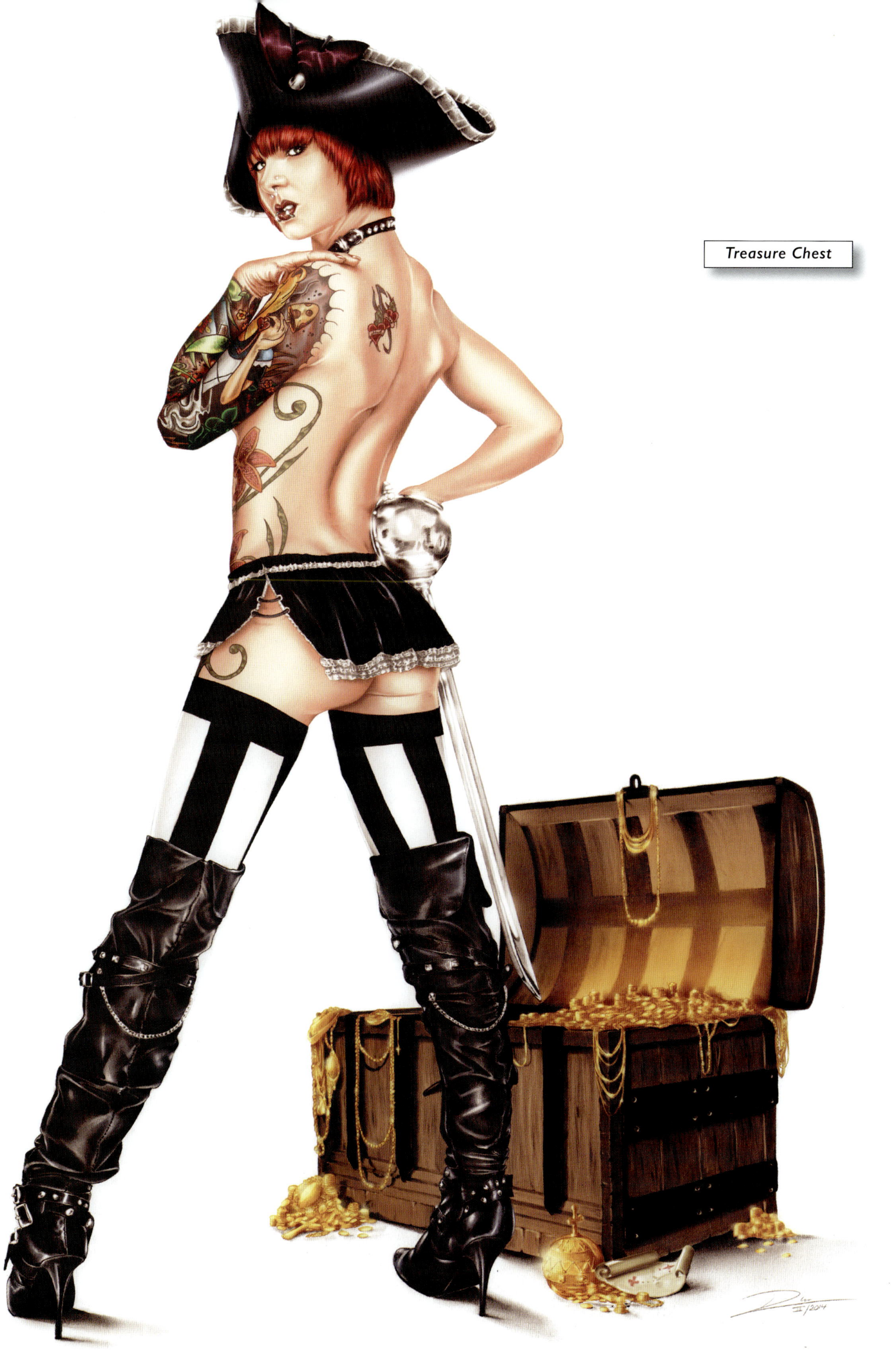

Treasure Chest

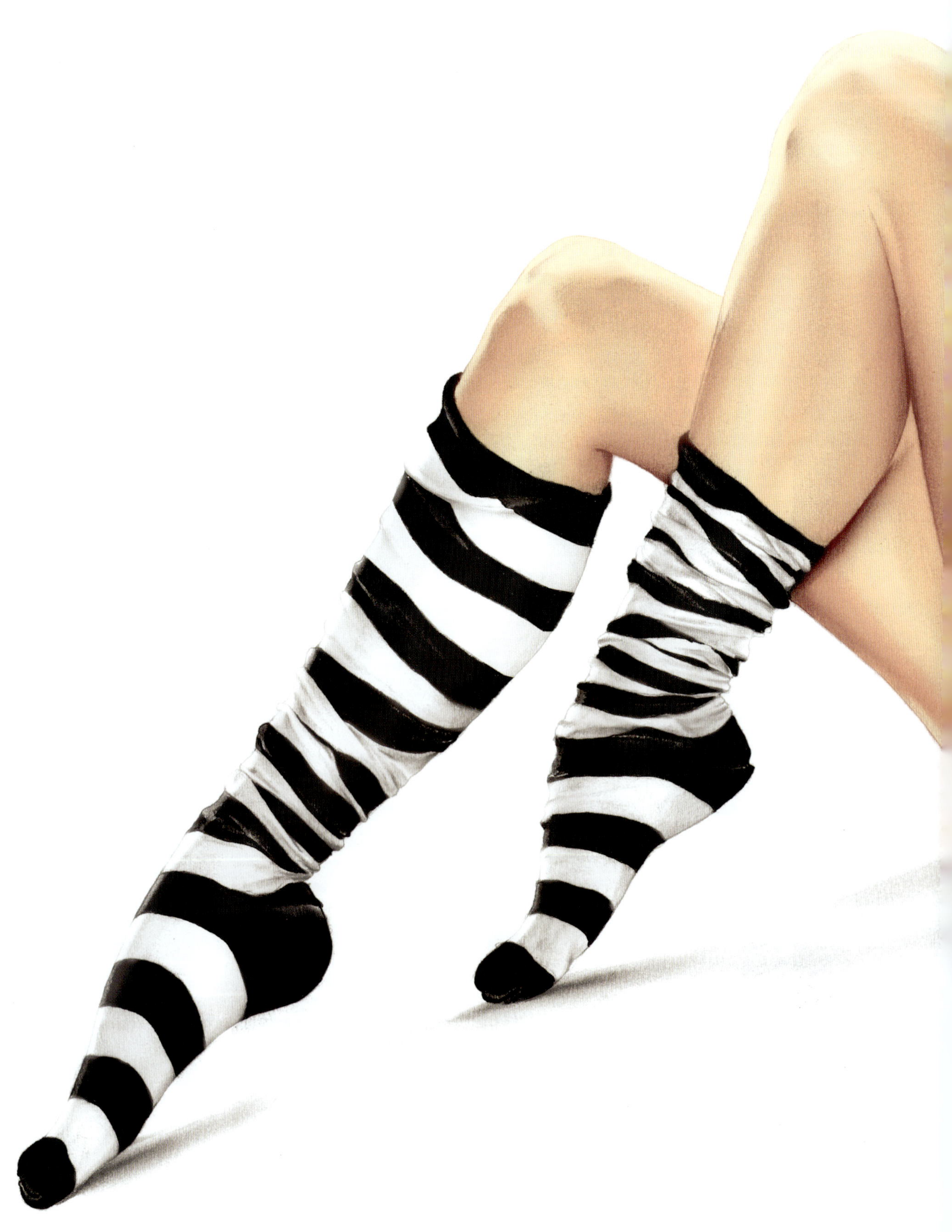

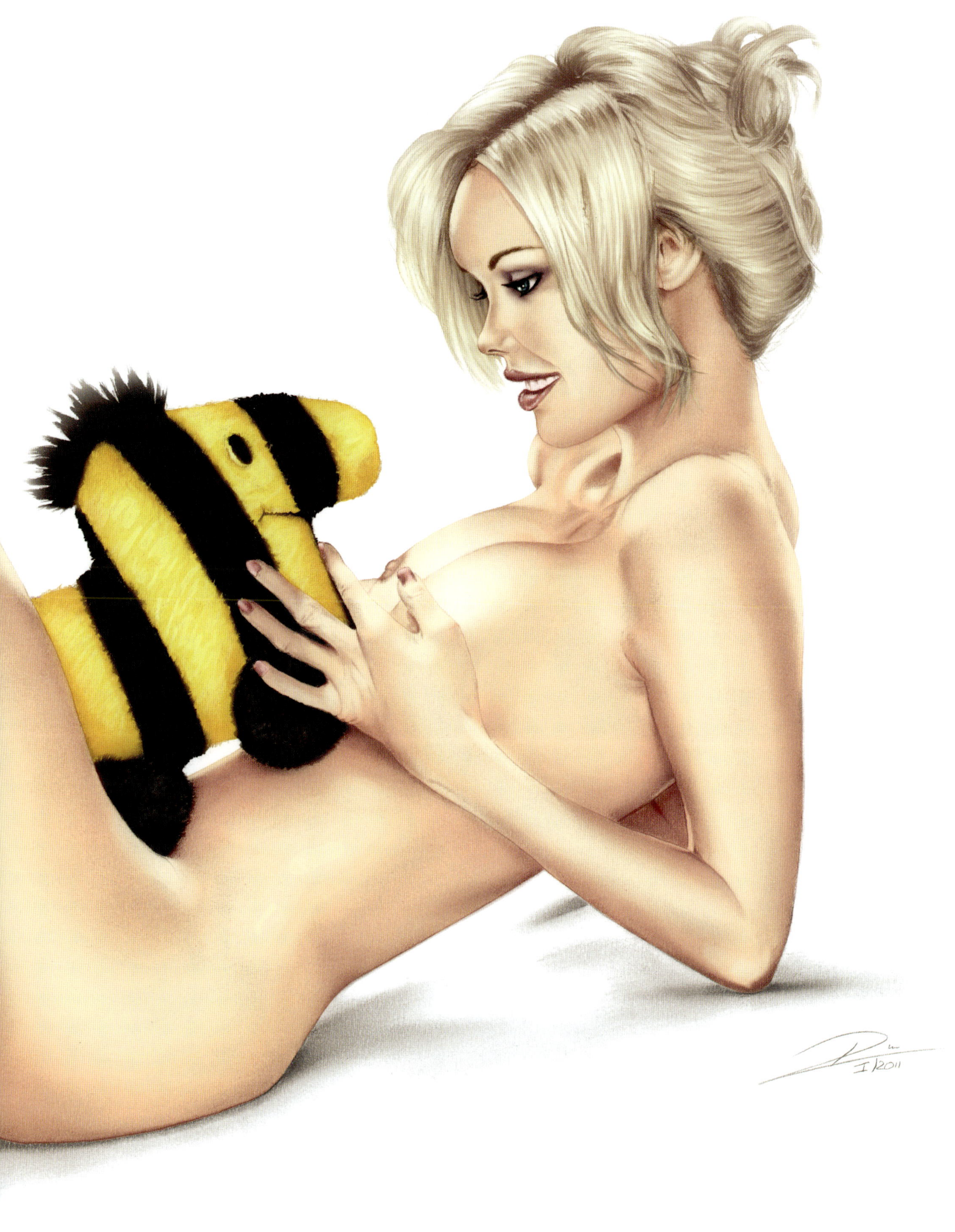

Tiger Ducky

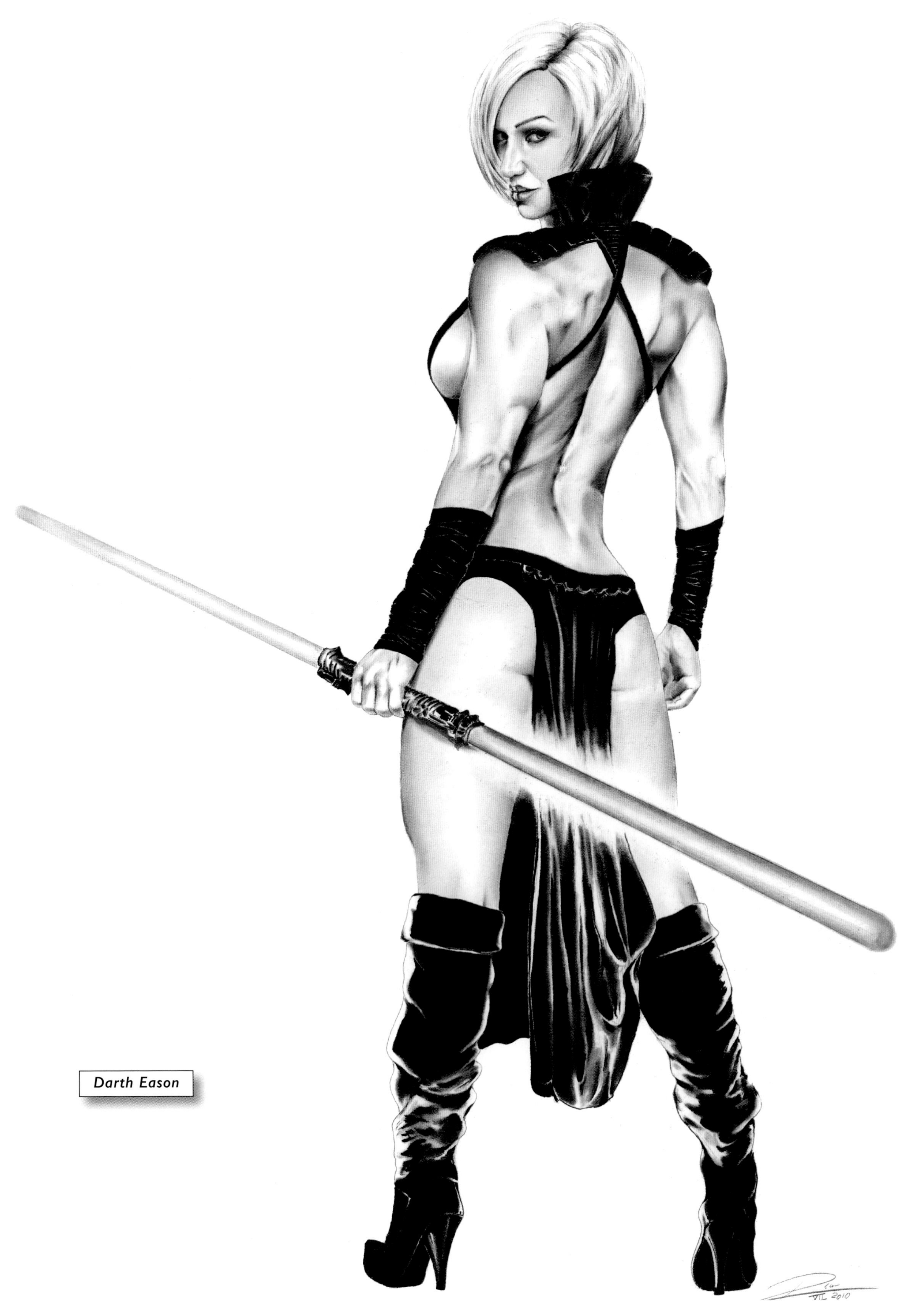

Darth Eason

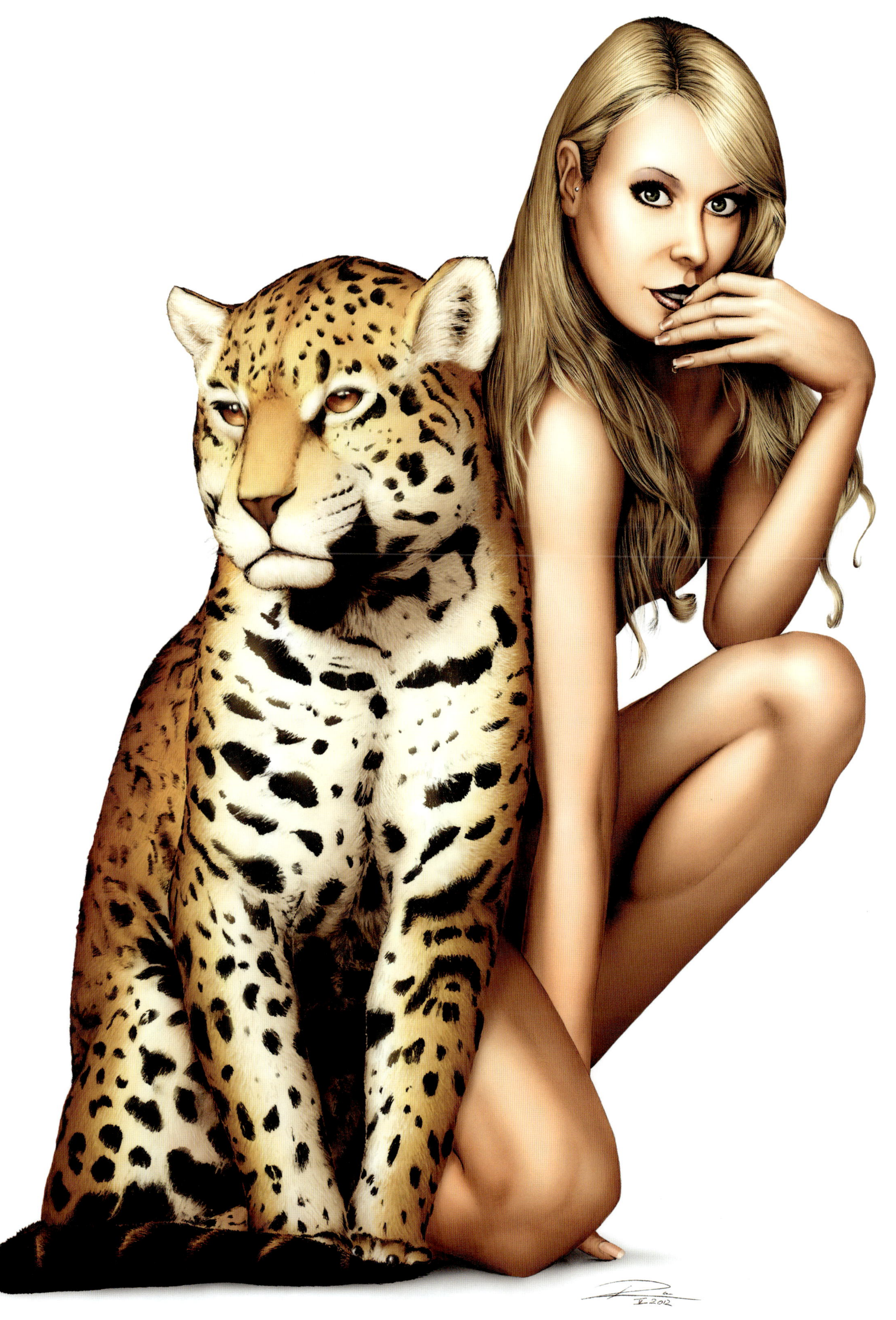

Untamed Beauties

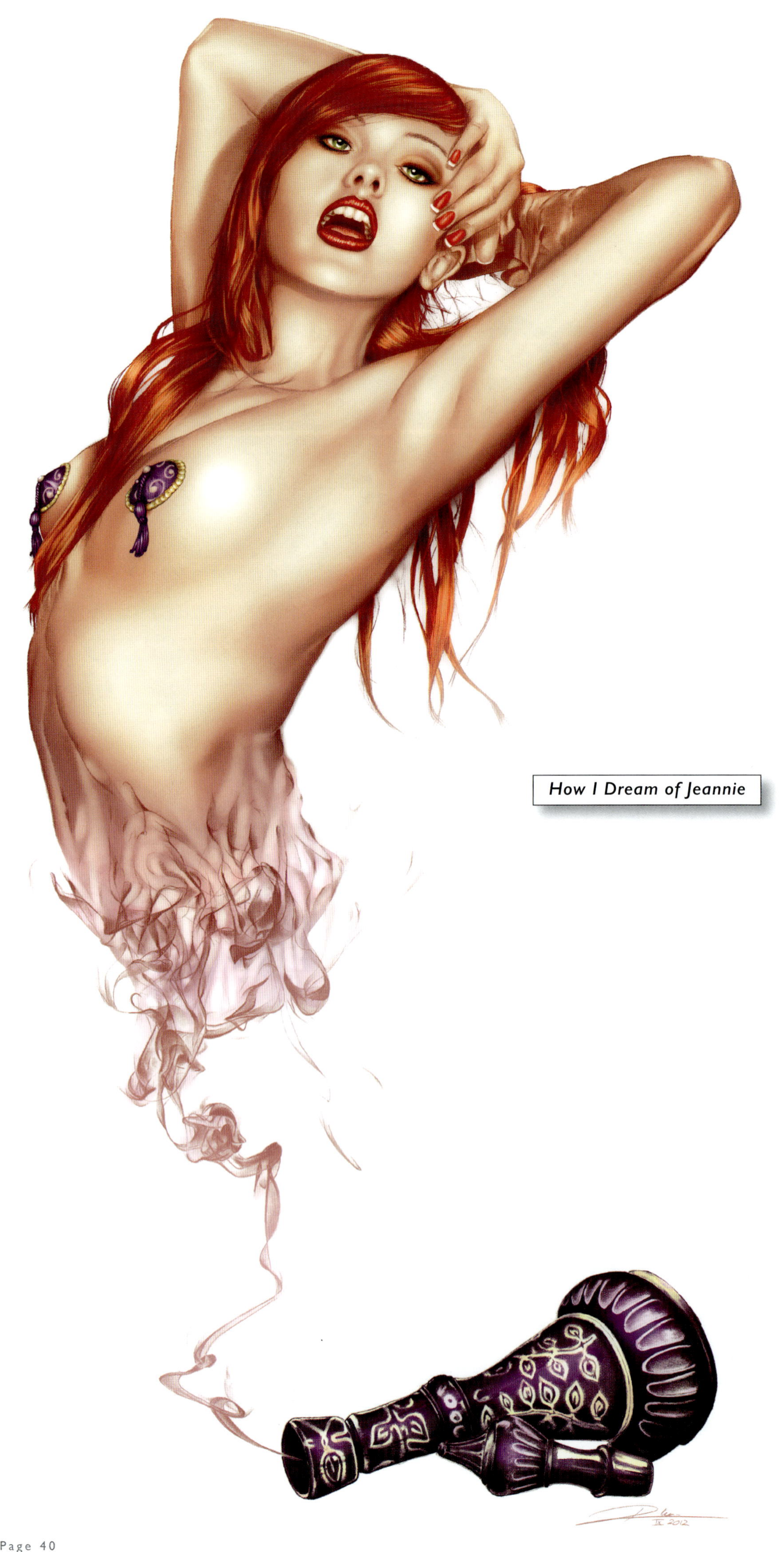

How I Dream of Jeannie

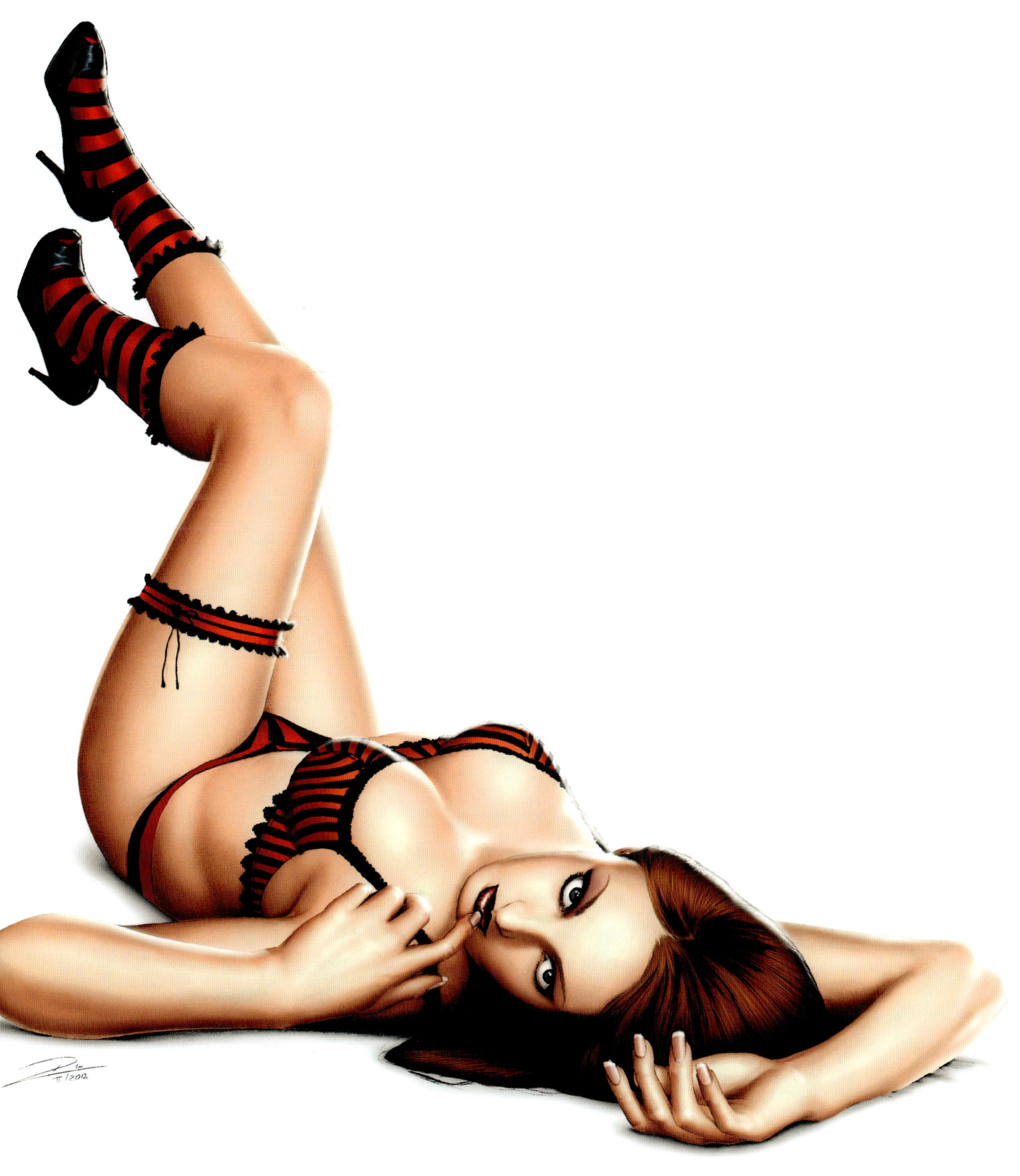

Vintage Stripes

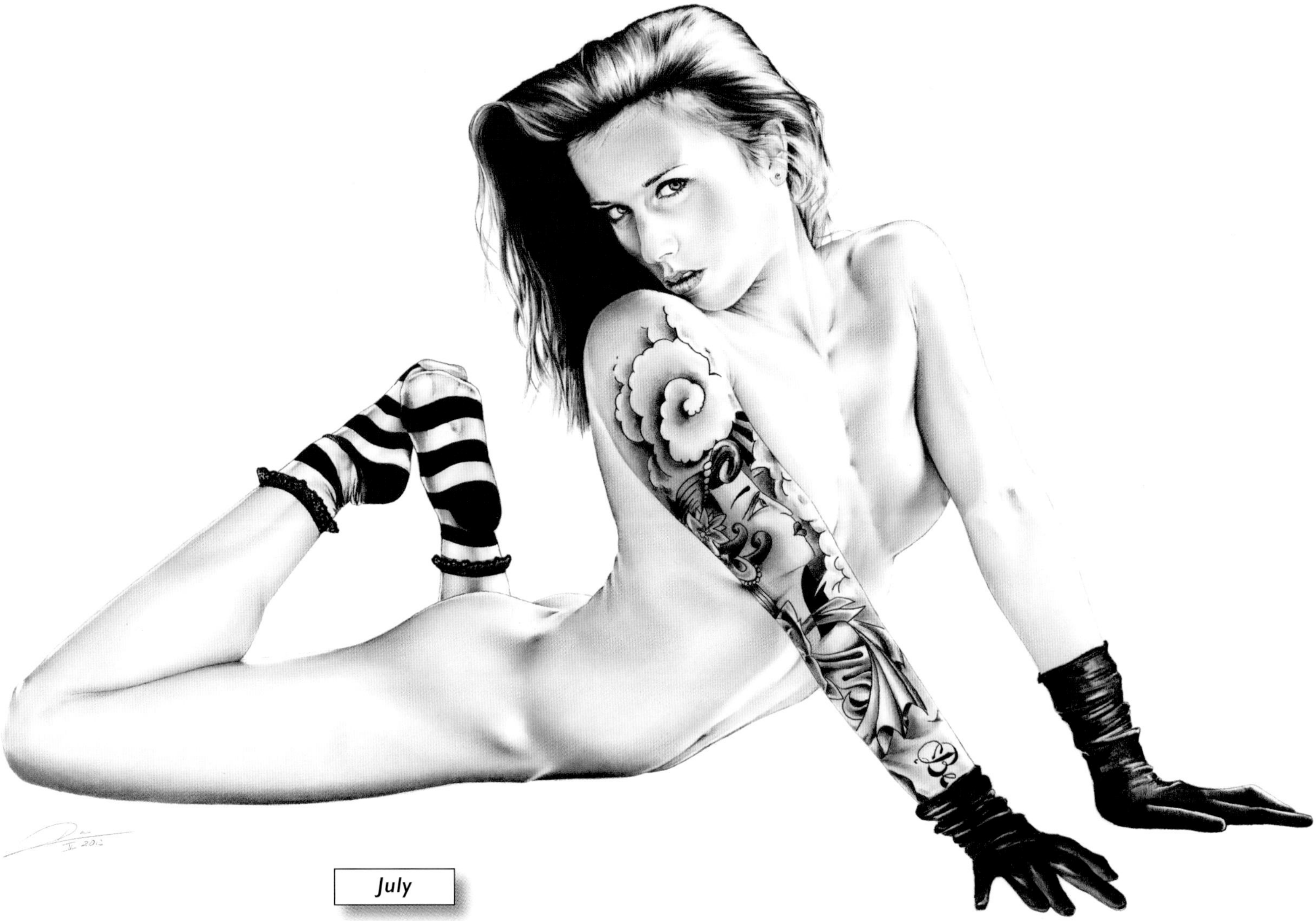

July

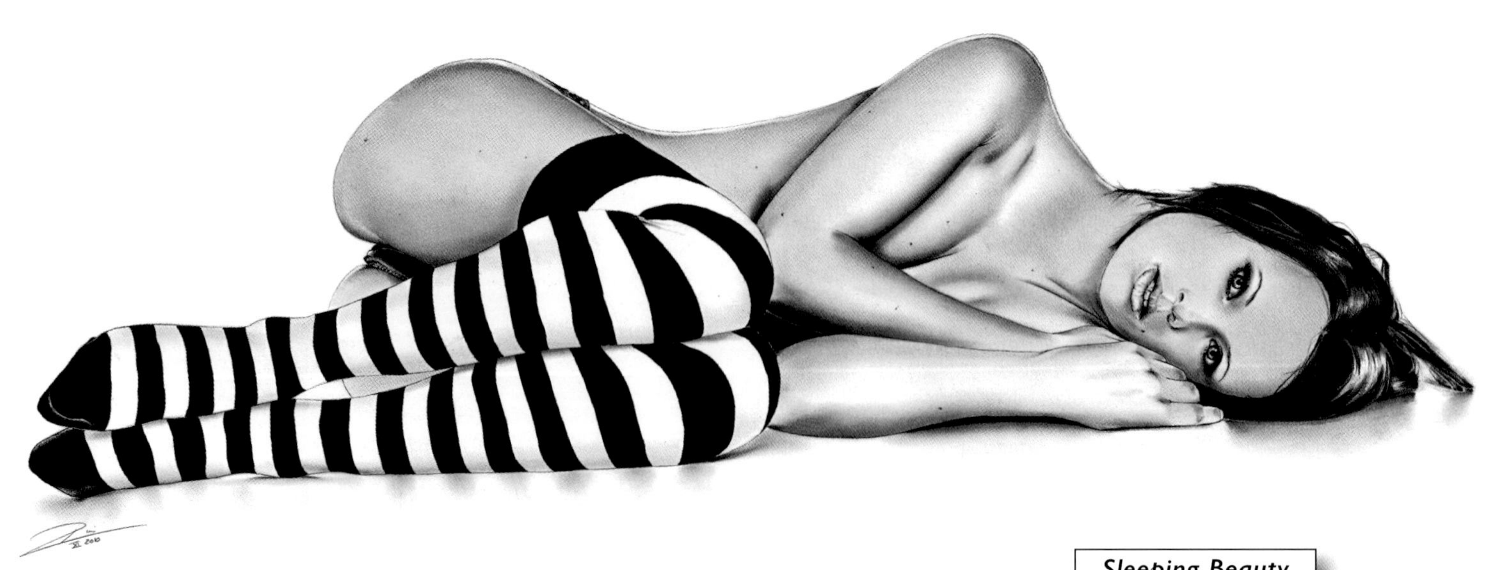

Sleeping Beauty

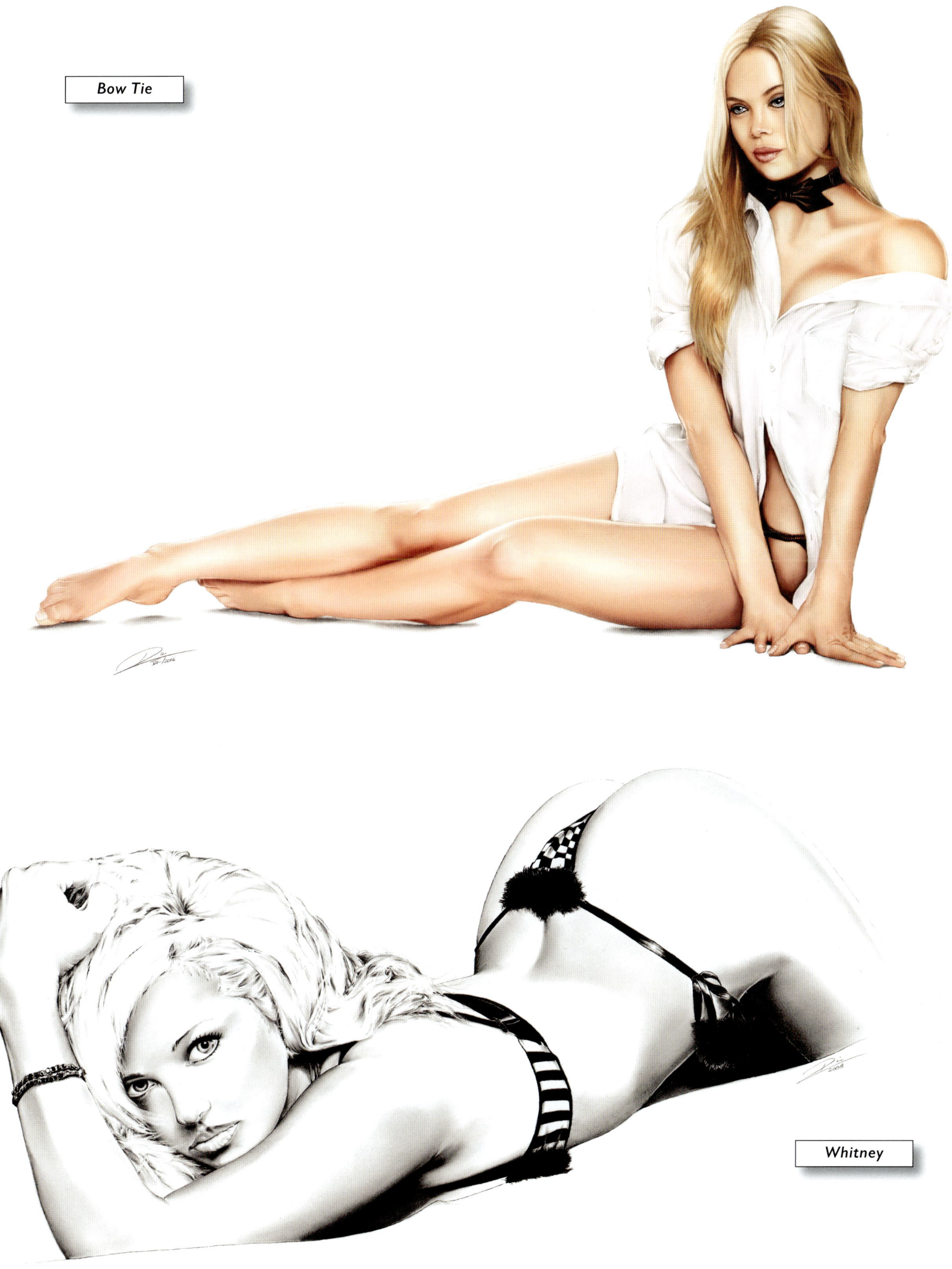

Bow Tie

Whitney

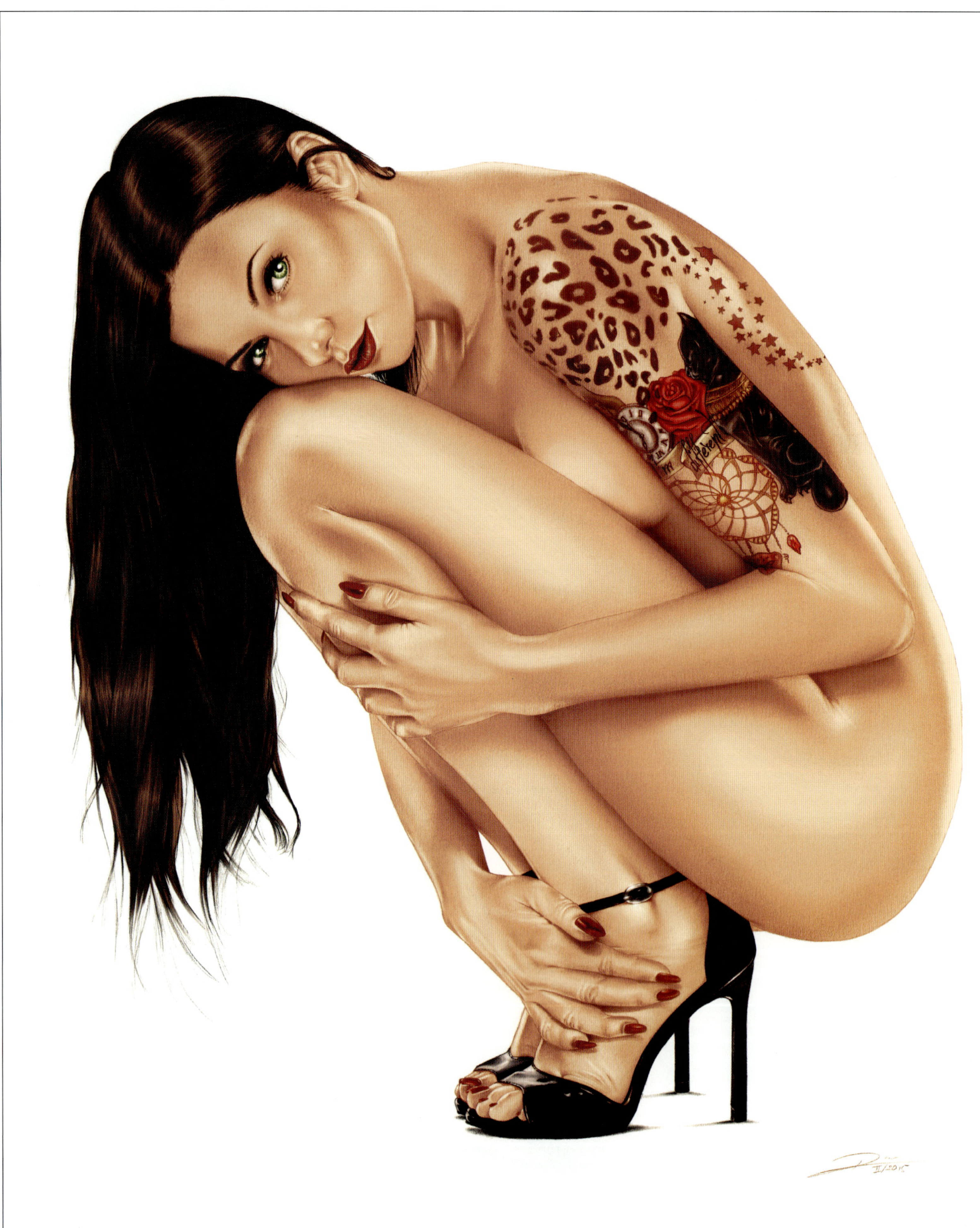

Shy Kitty

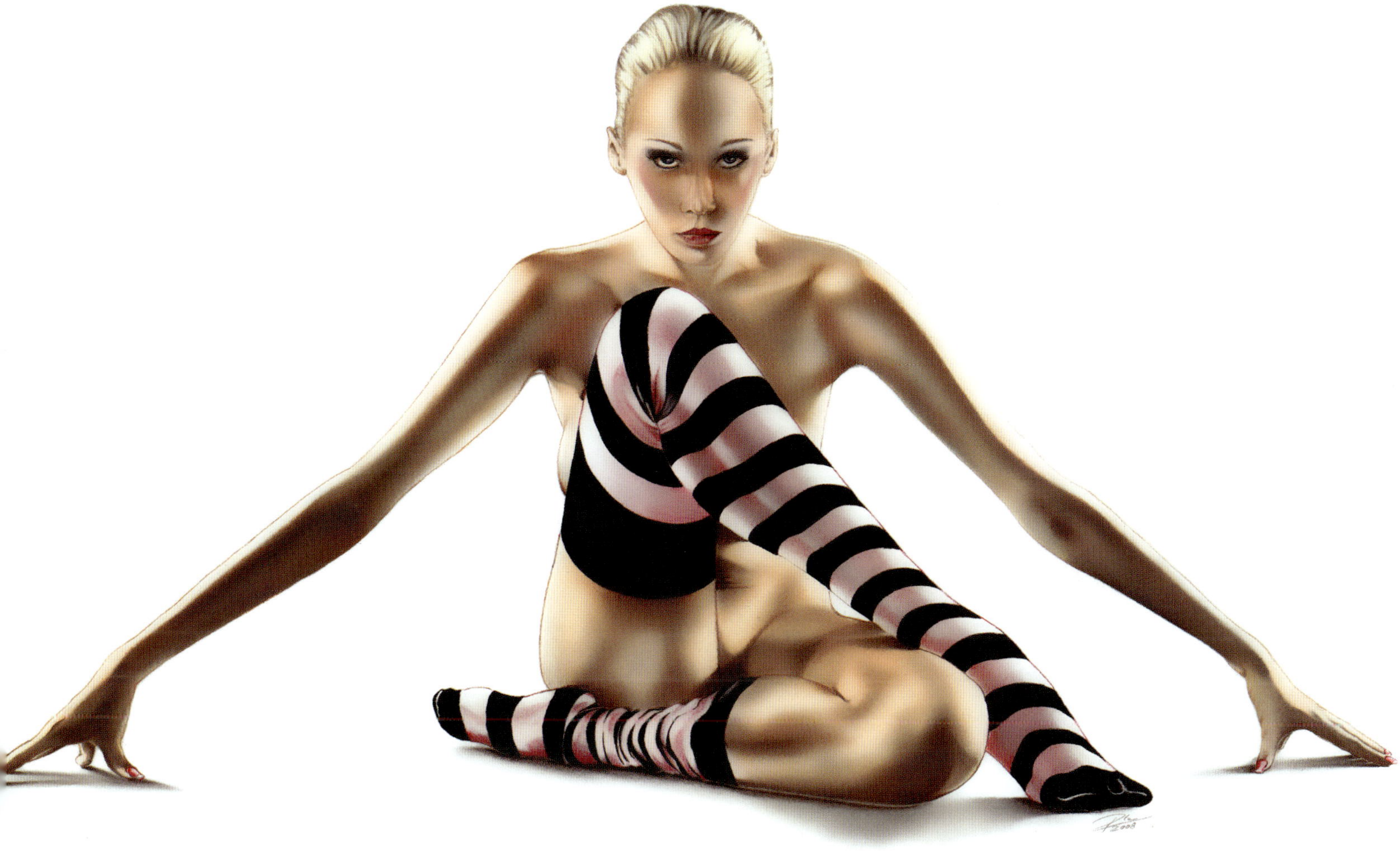

Albatross

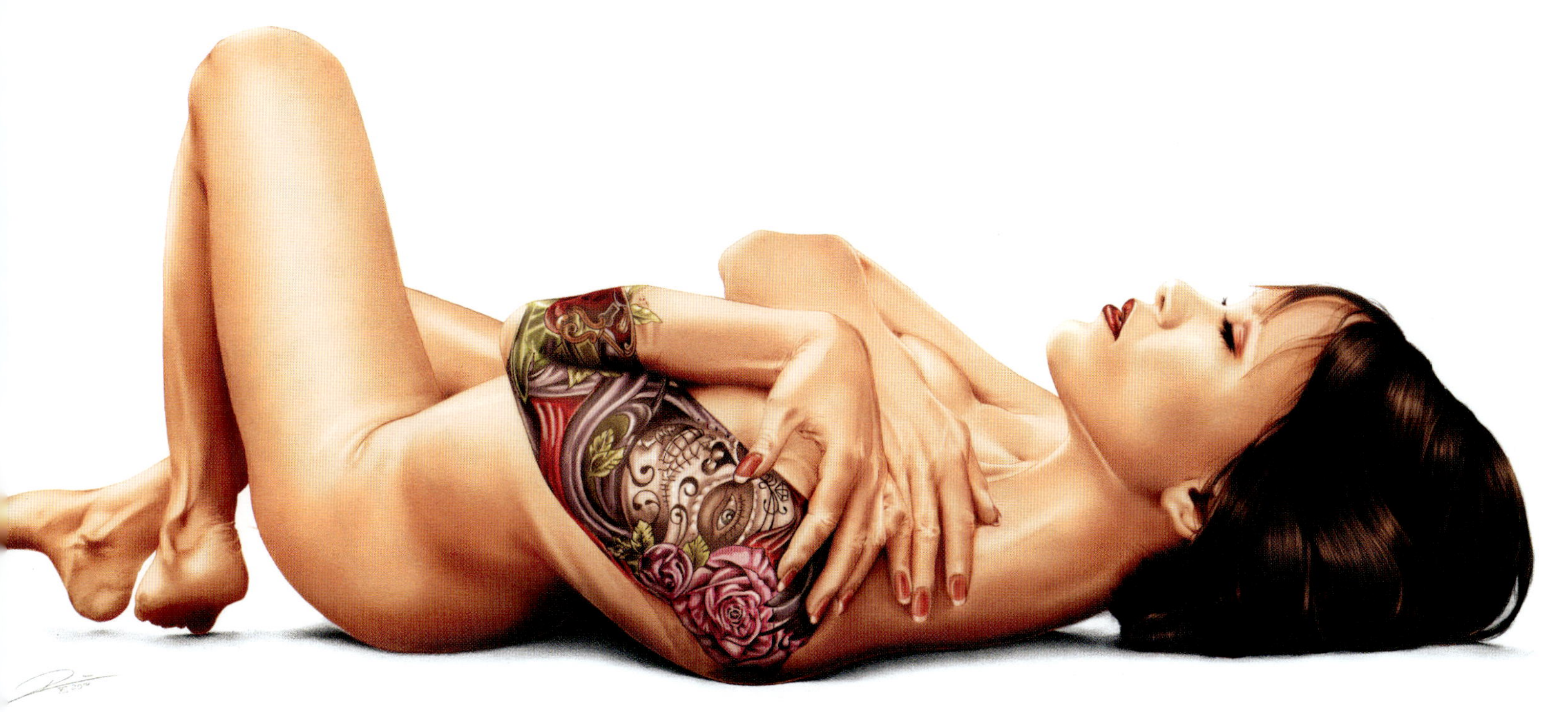

Sanctums Birth

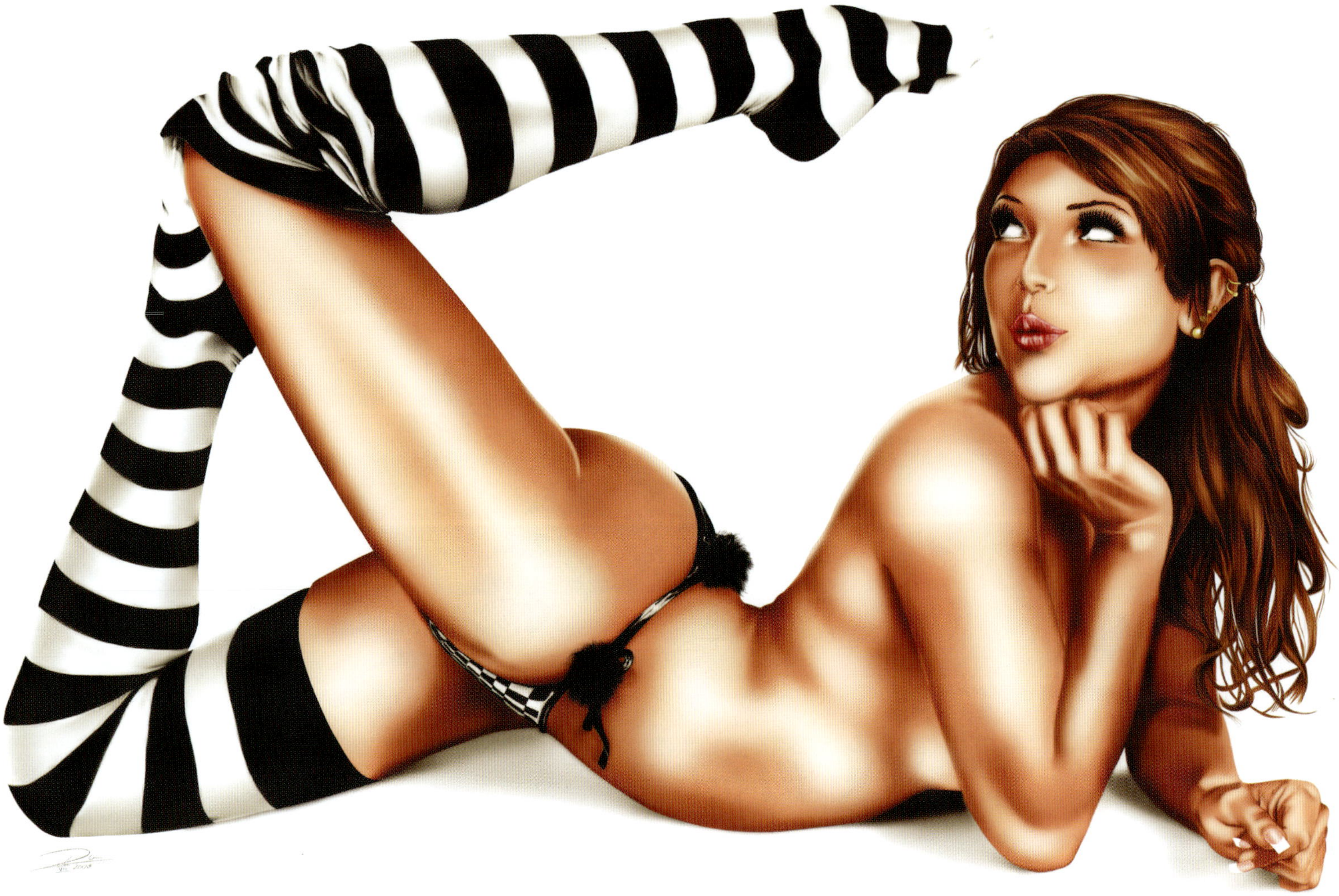

Strike A Pose

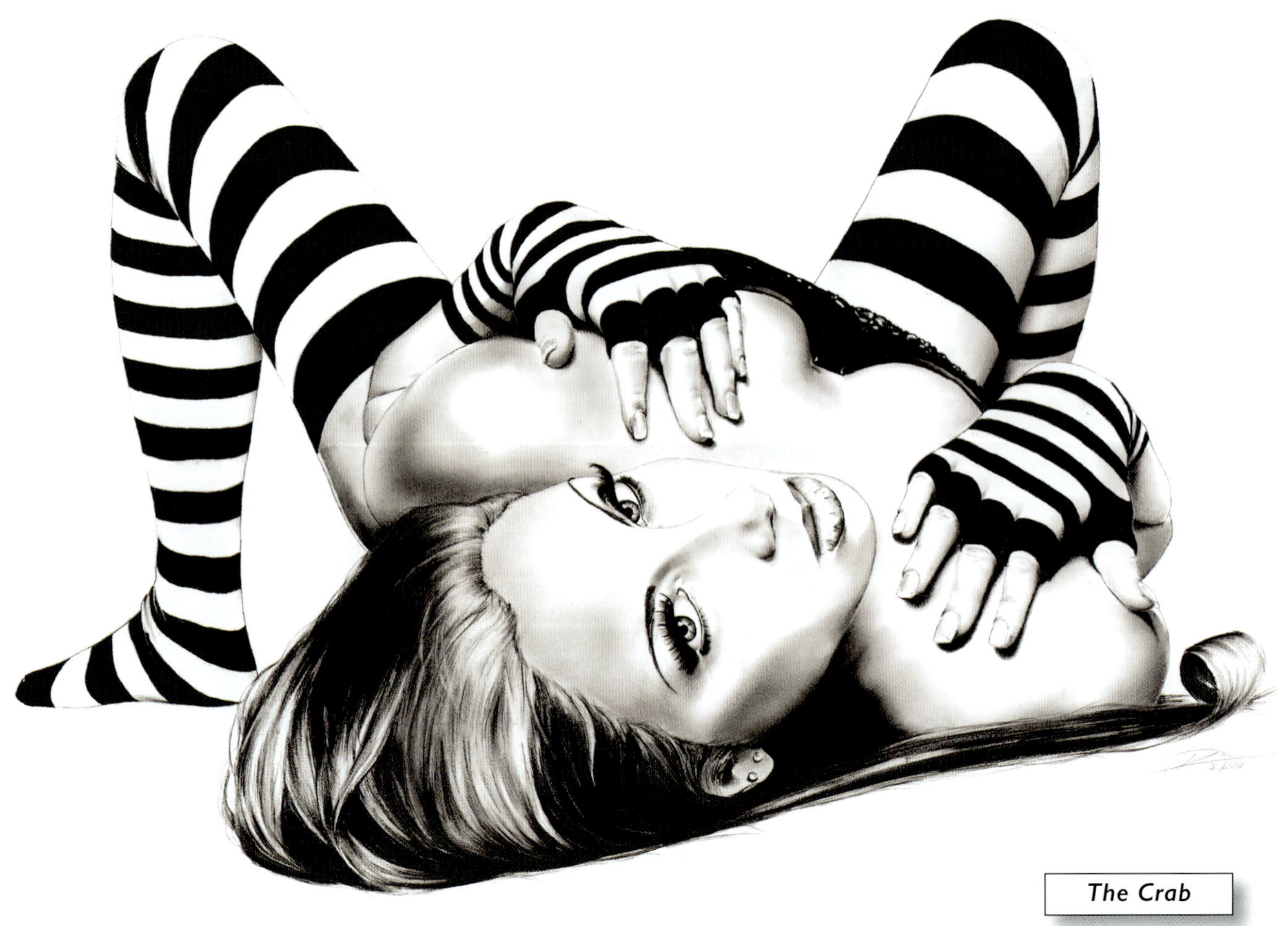

The Crab

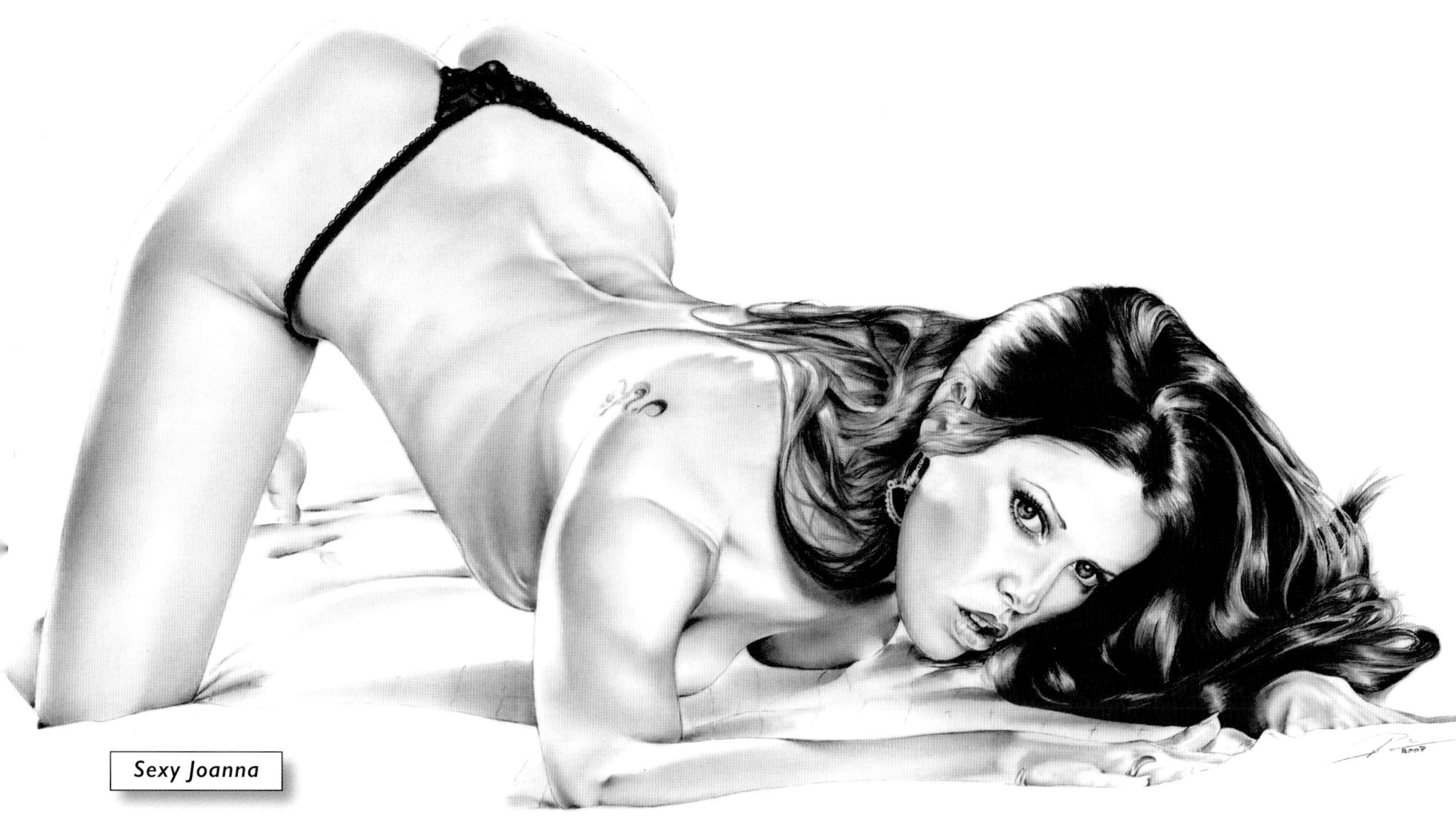

Sexy Joanna

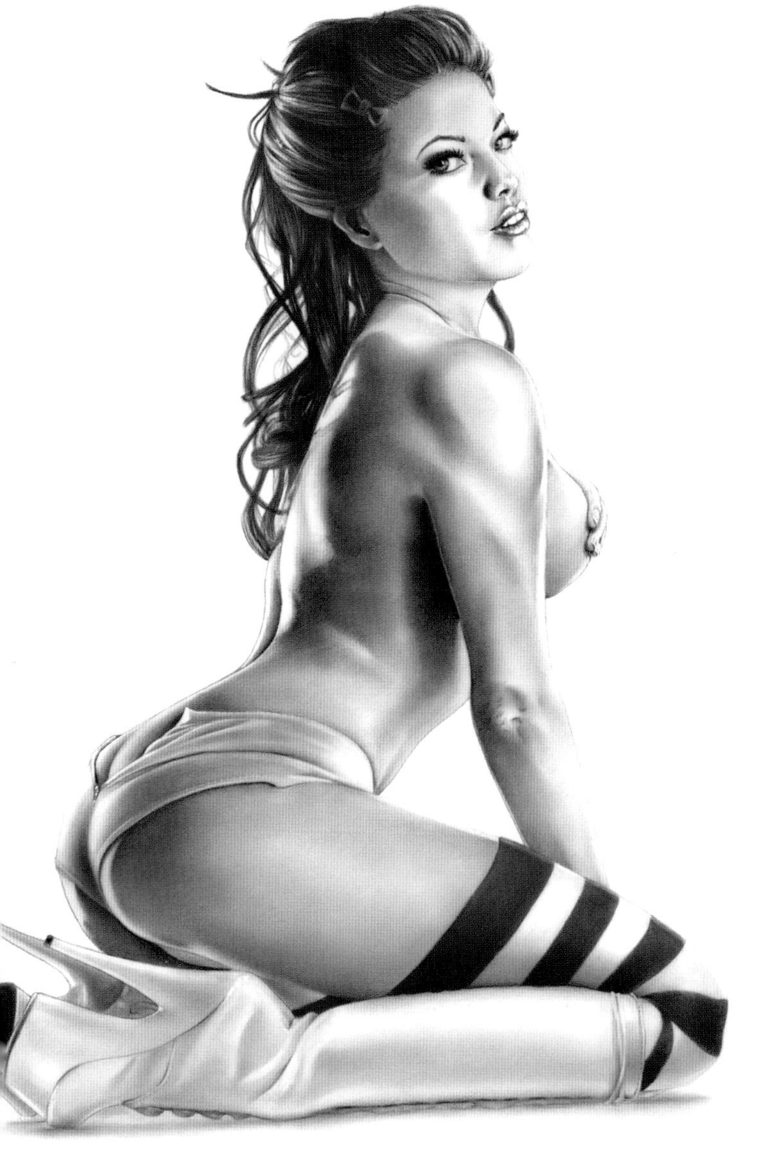

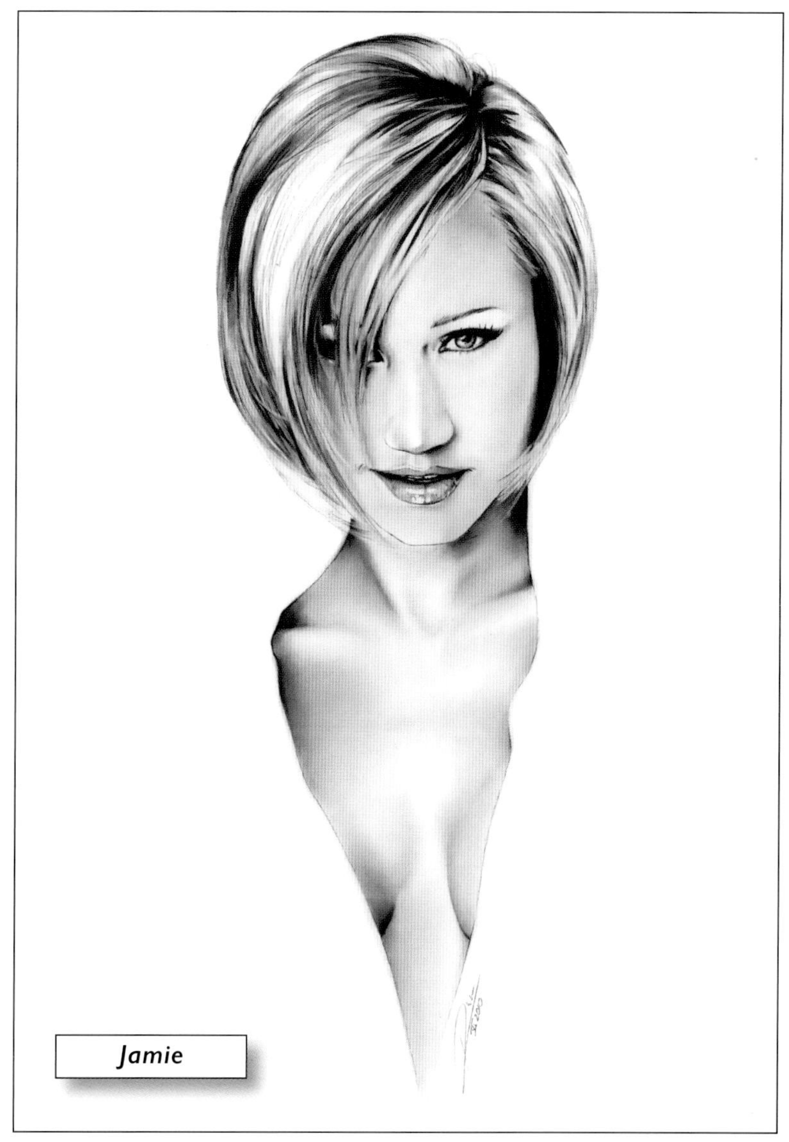

Jamie

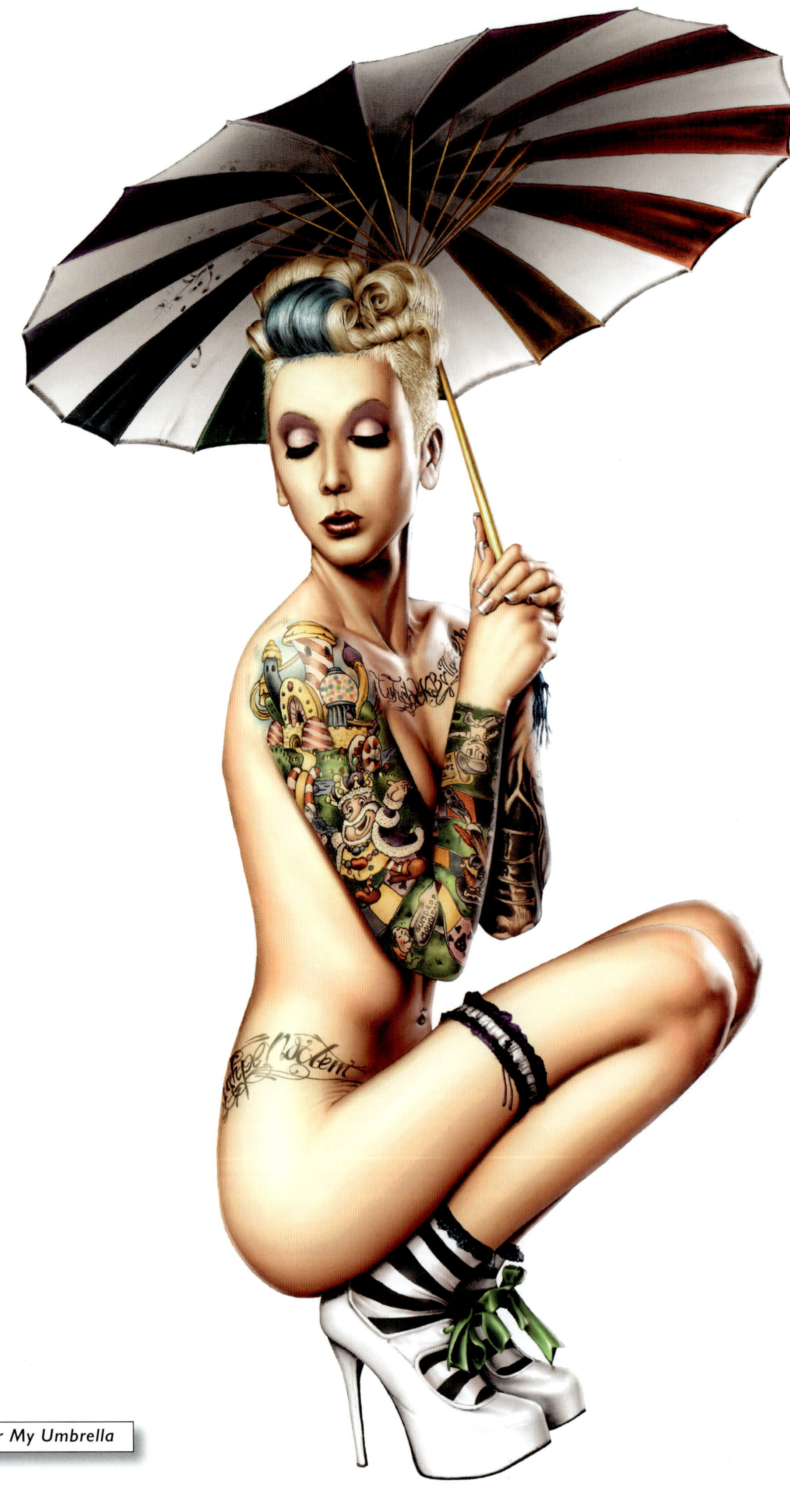

Under My Umbrella